WALKING

THE TAR PIT

KARIN SCHWAN

ISBN 978-1-0980-3117-6 (paperback)
ISBN 978-1-0980-3119-0 (hardcover)
ISBN 978-1-0980-3118-3 (digital)

Christian Faith Publishing, Inc.
832 Park Avenue
Meadville, PA 16335
www.christianfaithpublishing.com

Printed in the United States of America

PREFACE

This book is a collection of my thoughts and feelings put into words as I walked through what I call the Tar Pit. I named the grief process "the Tar Pit" years before Fred was diagnosed with brain cancer. In the nearly forty-year span of my nursing career, I used the term to describe the grief process to the numerous patients for which I was honored to care. I found describing it to people made it more tangible, and we could talk about the issues they were facing as it related to grieving, whether it be a loss through death or divorce, the loss of a job or a pet, or something else. Almost without fail, as I described my understanding of the Tar Pit, a look would come over that person that they understood what I was talking about, and it was how they felt about it too. Many times, they had been unable to put it into words. I never expected that I would be sitting smack in the middle of my Tar Pit by September 2016, a new widow at barely age fifty-five, having said goodbye to the man I loved so dearly. We had planned to celebrate at least fifty years of marriage, if not more. To say that life did not turn out as expected is an understatement!

I do not claim to be an expert on grief, though I do think I am an expert on *my* grief. And while I do not understand everyone's Tar Pit, I have gotten pretty good at navigating around my own. I have learned that while all of us have different Tar Pit experiences, we all have been, are currently in, or will soon find ourselves surrounded by…the Tar Pit.

When Fred was diagnosed with Glioblastoma, a very aggressive form of brain cancer, in May of 2016, I knew immediately how it was going to end. I was hopeful and prayerful and knew that God could and would cure Fred if it was His will. I prayed that Fred and I would have the strength to get through whatever God put before us. God did not disappoint. I simply could not have gotten through each day without the strength He provided to me and Fred through our family and friends. A quote by Marvin Williams sums it up: "God sends vertical help by horizontal means. He sends us what we need through the help of others." That was certainly true for us and continues for me still.

As I shared my thoughts and our story on Facebook, I received numerous comments from people asking me to keep writing because my "online journaling" touched them deeply. I was not prepared for this feedback, and as I heard from others in the Tar Pit, I was moved at how we all need each other for support to keep going. I believe that is the work of the Holy Spirit as He brings us together in fellowship and support.

While it was not the plan when I started writing after Fred was diagnosed, I was asked by several people if I was going to write a book. As time passed by after he died, I felt the need to continue writing. I wrote quite a bit as a young teenager and through my early twenties. The genre was primarily poetry, but I did dabble in short stories and essays. It was cathartic for me then, and I found comfort in writing during Fred's battle with "the Dragon" (glioblastoma). Writing has continued to offer an outlet for dealing with my grief since his death. Usually I had a box of tissues by my side and a plastic bag and hand gel as well to make it easier to keep myself gathered together as I wrote during the first two years. (For those who know me, I am a bit of a germaphobe and a nurse, so washing hands after blowing a nose is a must.) I am doing better now with the crying and not going through nearly as many tissues or bottles of hand gel.

This book is a culmination of my thoughts and feelings, essays, and letters from Fred's diagnosis and throughout the first two years after his death. The section containing Facebook posts start at the beginning of Fred's diagnosis through the first two years after he died. I have been inspired by so many people who have cheered me on, hugged me, or watched me cry while standing patiently by my side. I give a special thanks to Bryn Kaufman who gave me support, encouragement, and guidance in getting this book published.

There is a section called "Open Letters" included in this book. The letters are to various people such as Fred, our sons, "our girls," other family members and friends. I wanted to openly share some of my thoughts and feelings regarding how their love and support have truly made me able to continue on the path through the Tar Pit.

In the section with Bible verses, quotes, and other resources, I share those words that brought me comfort and continue to do so. Many times, I read them in the wee hours of the night when I could not sleep because my heart was so heavy or I could not turn off all the thoughts scrambling in my brain at the time. Some of the verses were part of my daily devotionals, and it is uncanny how they seemed perfectly placed on that day. They were exactly the words I needed to read and hold in my heart.

And finally, I include in this book the eulogy I wrote as I kept a bedside vigil during the last days of Fred's earthly life. Boy, did I go through the tissues and hand gel! This is the eulogy I read at Fred's funeral. I am not sure I could replicate those words if I sat down again to write them. I truly feel the Holy Spirit gave me the strength and ability to write them and, certainly, the strength to stand before hundreds of people at Fred's funeral to speak them.

I hope the emoting of this quirky widow lady brings hope, peace and, yes, some laughs as you read this book. I also hope that you feel the grace and mercy of God as you read it, for if it were not for those, I simply would not be able to walk the path to the other side of the Tar Pit.

The Diagnosis

Fred and I always talked about traveling to Australia and New Zealand. We were avid travelers and traveled exceptionally well together; not all couples are able to do this. For many couples who travel, the end result causes more stress than the trip is intended to diffuse. Fred and I destressed throughout our many, many trips together, and it was a wonderful way to reset and rekindle our relationship. We both led very busy lives in our jobs, and sometimes a much-anticipated trip was the only thing that kept us going.

April 2016 was the long-awaited trip to Australia; instead of also going New Zealand, the add-on was Fiji. We never thought of going there, but the trip was a package deal, and Australia/Fiji would be our "bucket list" trip. It would particularly special as we would be in Fiji for Fred's sixty-third birthday.

The trip was wonderful, though the travel to and from Australia/ Fiji was exhausting and a bit brutal for us. We snorkeled at the Great Barrier Reef, climbed the famous Sidney Harbor Bridge, took a Skyway cable ride through the rainforest and up to Kuranda, and visited Hartley's Crocodile Adventure, where I got to hold a koala. We walked all over Cairns and Sydney. We spent time in Fiji walking along the beach and took a little sail boat ride with a private guide out into the Pacific Ocean for several hours.

On Fred's birthday, I surprised him by renting an ocean-side hut, and we had a delicious gourmet dinner watching the most beautiful sunset we had ever seen. In fact, the sunset was so spectacular that lifelong island residents commented that they had never seen a sunset so spectacular. I took multiple pictures all along the trip and particularly of that spectacular sunset to forever capture the moment. I nearly dragged Fred out of bed early the next day to walk to the optimal sight to get sunrise pictures on our last day on the island. We had a long and arduous trip home before us.

During the trip, Fred was tired, but then again, so was I. We had scrambled prior to leaving for the trip to get many things completed in preparation for being gone. The timing was not good for the lawn and landscape business. April is usually the beginning of a rapid grass growth period. Leaving work for me was always stressful as I always had so much to come back to upon my return. And yet we both dug in, got caught up, and were so excited for our trip of a lifetime together.

On the trip, we laughed and talked of my upcoming "retirement" plan. I was turning fifty-five at the end of July and could officially retire from the hospital. June 2016 would be thirty-four years of service, and our plan was that I would retire on August 1, 2016 and take a few months off to "relax." We both knew I would need to get another job but would take off a few months to see where the winds sent me in search of a new job. I would later plan for "real retirement" in my sixties.

For those who know me, I am known as a planner. I plan everything. I make lists, I check off my lists as I get things accomplished, and then I plan again. I had many, many plans for the future. One of the most important plans was that I would be married to Fred for at least fifty years—that seemed to be an incredibly important milestone for me. Here is what I know about my plans vs. God's plans; His plans *always* win in the end. For this girl, a control freak to the core, having someone else give me a plan that I had no choice but to actively participate in was a blow that brought me to my knees.

When we headed back from Fiji, Fred was overwhelmingly tired. I had noticed he was quite tired on the island, but I was tired too. Between the jet lag, constant activities, heat and humidity, it didn't surprise me or particularly concern me. We both knew he needed to lose weight, and between the weight and his blood pressure, we both thought those were additional factors in his fatigue. We decided he would see his primary care physician when we got back home.

We had a ten-plus hour layover in LAX (Los Angeles airport). It was a confusing location where we chose to wait the long hours and both of us got lost going to and from the bathroom. Fred was better at directions than just about anyone I have ever known, but the fact he got lost didn't concern me. I chalked it up to the fact that we both were so tired from travel. Once we got home though, the "misguided direction" issue continued. This was a man who knew every road in Ashland County and most in neighboring counties. He was struggling to find his way around the city of Ashland as he mowed customers' lawns he had taken care of for years. He told me he thought he had suffered a "plane stroke" as his memory issues were concerning him. I told him I didn't think he had a stroke but certainly he should see his primary care physician.

Dutifully, Fred made an appointment and saw his physician. He had no neurological deficits, but his blood pressure was a little elevated. Fred and his physician discussed his weight and getting more rest, and some lab work was ordered as well as a carotid doppler to check blood flow through his neck arteries just in case he had previously undetected blockage. The confusion seemed to lift, and we continued to work to get caught up from being gone.

Several days later, the entire family went to the zoo. Fred always lagged behind me when walking. Over the years of marriage, he learned to pick up his walking speed to keep up with me. We all noticed he was struggling to keep up with us as we ambled though the zoo with a four-year-old and a seven-month pregnant Michelle. Fred and I sat on a bench, resting while everyone else climbed through... yes, the Australia exhibit. Fred teared up and told me something was wrong, terribly wrong; he couldn't explain it, and I had never seen him this way. My heart sank to my toes; something was indeed wrong, and I didn't know what it was. This was a Saturday.

By the next Wednesday, we still did not know what the problem was, but the doppler test would be done soon, and maybe that would give us the answer. I remember the moment like it was yesterday. I was walking across the bedroom and stopped; my heart felt like it stopped too. "Brain tumor" came into my mind. "Oh my God, my Lord, please help us, Fred has a brain tumor" came rushing through my brain. It literally took my breath away; I could barely stand. I pulled out my phone, texted Fred's physician, and asked for a brain

MRI. I texted that I thought it was a brain tumor. Fred's dad died of a rare form of non-familial brain cancer in 1982. (It would turn out that Fred's dad's tumor was very different.)

Anyone who knows how medicine and insurance works these days knows that nothing moves fast in the outpatient world. There are precertifications to get done, the correct ICD-10 code to be entered, the insurance denials, the peer-to-peer appeals, etc. I assumed this would be no different; however, things moved more quickly due to some amazing teamwork at Fred's primary care physician office, and I am grateful. The brain MRI would be scheduled for Monday, May 9. Now we just needed to get through the weekend. It was Mother's Day weekend. Getting through the weekend was heavy and hard. Fred's condition rapidly declined to the point I could not leave him alone. He was confused and could barely walk. He was so unsteady on his feet that he had to hang onto the walls to walk and I had to hold him up on the stairs. I tried so hard to hold it together for him, for the family, and for me. I knew when I started to break down, I would probably not be able to reel it back in easily. The wait was excruciating, but I really already knew the diagnosis; my prayer was that it was an operable, non-malignant brain tumor and we would get through this. I had a plan—fifty years of marriage with my man.

Monday morning came, and I had a full schedule of patients in the physician's office where I worked on Mondays. My mom and Fred's sister, Barb, would take him to the hospital for his MRI. I watched the clock between patients as the time for the MRI loomed. Less than an hour after the MRI was scheduled, my phone rang at the office. It was Fred's physician; the news was devastating.

"Karin, this is bad, the mass is huge and deep and it looks like a glioblastoma. Where do you want me arrange for Fred to go? How soon can you get him there?"

My head was spinning and I felt like I had been sucker punched. I literally could not breathe. I felt my knees buckle. "Oh my God, my Lord, please help us, how will we get through this?" Before I knew it, the office staff was helping me get out the door to come home and pick up Fred and head to Columbus to the OSU James Cancer Center. Nicolaus met us at the house to tell his dad that he had been called by Ashland Fire Department and offered a position as firefighter/paramedic at the same department Fred worked for over thirty years and retired as captain. While Fred was confused, he was able to comprehend Nicolaus's news. Wow, what a contrast in joy and deep, horrible shock!

We quickly moved to the car and headed South to Columbus. Fred couldn't understand what was happening, I could barely breathe and was concentrating on driving to a place I had only been one other time. Thankfully, GPS was available, and we arrived in just over an hour to the front door. The navigation to the oncology neurology department began with me having no idea where I was going with a confused man who was nearly oblivious to what was going on. The wait to see the oncologist seemed like days. Each minute loomed; the air was heavy. "Oh my God, my Lord, help us. How will we get through this? I have a plan—fifty years with my man."

The neuro-oncologist was kind and sweet and direct. He knew that I was a nurse, and he quickly ascertained that Fred was confused and didn't really understand what was happening. He explained our situation, which was dire, yet he did give us some hope. I knew, though, that unless it was God's plan to give Fred a cure, this was going to end in a way none of us wanted. Most people do not survive glioblastoma, and if they do, it is not for long and the neurological deficits are devastating for all involved. Our only hope was to do a biopsy for confirmation and start chemotherapy and radiation as soon as possible.

Thus, "the diagnosis" was upon us. After Fred was admitted to his room, I began making the phone calls to family and, most importantly, "our boys." It was so hard to be away from them and try to not sob uncontrollably. The last thing they needed, or me for that matter, was to go over the cliff now when being strong was really the only option. I was on my knees and God was by my side; it was time to pull up my "Big Girl panties," wipe the tears, and face the diagnosis. Fred needed me strong, and he had been my rock for so many years it was my turn to be his.

I try to not replay the day of the diagnosis too often as it is still overwhelming painful. Just the thought of that day still takes my breath away. I am not sure I will ever get over that feeling. It is interesting though; it has given me perspective. Now I find things that would have normally made me angry, irritated, or overwhelmed generally just make me take a deep breath. I tell myself, "Well, I have certainly been through worse, I'll make it through this," and God will always be by my side.

Walking the Path through the Tar Pit
(A Journey Should Involve Plane Tickets to a Fun Destination)

I have often heard "the cancer journey" when referring to the experience of dealing with cancer. I refuse to call it a journey because a journey should be fun and involve something I look forward to doing which usually also involves plane tickets. The experience Fred and I and our family embarked on in May of 2016 was anything but fun; we named it our cancer path or "the path" for short.

Our family enjoyed, and still does today, hiking. Over the years, Fred and I, then the boys, have hiked all over the United States and internationally. Generally, the hikes have been on marked trails made to protect the fragile environment and to keep people from wandering off into unknown danger. When hiking and coming to an overgrown path, it is a sign that it is either less traveled or that it shouldn't be used for travel at all. Yes, I know Robert Frost wrote an entire poem about "the road less traveled," but his wasn't a path. I wasn't looking forward to the cancer path we had just been dropped onto, and I knew I would much rather be hiking. God has a funny way of putting us where He wants us regardless of our plan. (Remember, I still have this fifty-year plan of being married to Fred, and I was hanging onto it tightly.)

Almost as soon as Fred was admitted to the James Cancer Center, he had intravenous steroids which started to reduce the swelling in the brain. The tumor was quite large, called a "space-occupying lesion." The skull does not expand, so as the brain swells from injury or a space-occupying lesion, the risk of seizure activity is quite high. The physicians were amazed that Fred had not had a seizure due to the size of the tumor. The symptoms of his confusion and a near inability to walk were directly related to the increasing pressure and swelling in his brain. The hope was that the steroids would work to reduce the swelling and improve his symptoms. It was amazing, but by that evening, I began to see improvements in Fred's cognitive ability, his speech, swallowing, and his mobility.

As I kept a bedside vigil, Fred and I talked, laughed, and cried about our life together. We reflected on how lucky we were to find one another and how blessed we had been in keeping our marriage together despite the high percentage of firefighters who have marriages that end in divorce. Fred and I knew we were incredibly blessed with two truly wonderful sons who had found their life partners. We had one adorable and loving granddaughter, and had another on the way, due in August. We talked about how much we each knew that we were loved by the other and how, no matter "how this turned out," we had been given so much more in life that we deserved. God was good despite the walls crumbling around our piece of utopia.

It was stunning actually. We had just gotten back from a trip of a lifetime. We snorkeled amongst large fish and coral and climbed to the top of the Sydney Harbor Bridge. (Oh my God, My Lord, thank you that we made it through all our travels without Fred having a seizure.) What a blessing and gift! Of all the things I have dealt with in many years of nursing, I found dealing with seizures to be the thing I really dreaded. For some reason, watching someone seize has always bothered me, and how lucky we were that Fred did not have a seizure while on the trip or while driving.

Fred and I talked that first night at the James about how we wanted to let people know about the brain tumor and what was happening. We did not want the rumor mill to be the source of truth. We had lost control of so much of what was happening that we wanted to control the facts. Both of us were on Facebook but mostly for funny things and sharing pictures. We weren't using it for deeply personal situations, and yet we thought it would be a way to reach quite a few people and keep them updated. And so it began—my Facebook posts from the Tar Pit.

As a nurse, especially as a critical care nurse, and then as a nurse practitioner, I had many opportunities to be with people in their darkest moments. I call it an opportunity, because to be allowed into something so personal as an individual's grief is to be honored and trusted. I counseled quite a few people in family practice dealing with unresolved grief, and rarely did I prescribe a pill to fix the issue.

In my discussions with patients, I likened the grieving process to a tar pit. It is thick, dark and heavy. It is difficult to trudge through, and at times, pulls you under and almost suffocates you. To successfully navigate the Tar Pit, you have to actually get into the pit. You cannot, no matter how hard you try, avoid getting in if you are to get through the grief. Some just dip their toes in the pit, some jump in with full force, and some slowly wade in. No matter how you get in, the bottom line is you must get into it if you are ever to get through it. You cannot go around it or over it.

There are some who refuse to ever enter the Tar Pit. To me, that isn't unresolved grief; it is unrecognized grief in the form of denial. When this happens, the person will never be able to resolve their grief. It will hang on them like a heavy weight forever, and it often is dealt with by self-destructive behaviors of self-medication: food, drugs, alcohol, sex, isolation, etc.

Some get into the Tar Pit and begin a forward progression only to be stopped by distractions. Sometimes the person flounders for a while and then gets back into a forward movement. Rarely do people keep moving forward in a steady and continuous motion. Those that do are fortunate as I haven't found that to be the case very often, and it certainly hasn't been for me. I think, generally, it is a stuttering and staggering forward motion with periods of being pulled back and pulled under. We may be pulled under by an additional loss such as that of another loved one or a financial loss. However, sometimes it is something small that triggers a much larger wave of tar that overcomes us. I found that to be the situation with me. It was usually a small event, a flat tire or something I couldn't find that I was looking for, that sent me into a downward spiral deep into the Tar Pit. It was quickly followed by a feeling of despair.

What I have learned in over a year in the Tar Pit, and actually more if you count the time from Fred's diagnosis until the current time, is that you just have to get in and start trudging along. It will never, ever get better if you don't get started. It isn't easy. It is messy, hard, and I hate it. I used to think it was like a lake and that you could see the other side once you got in. I quickly found out, as I was nearly drowning, that it is more like the ocean. A lake can have waves and be rough, but it is nothing like the ocean with larger waves and stronger undertows and more dangers lurking beneath the surface. Hum… I hadn't seen that coming as I really had never been so far out into the Tar Pit. Despite losing my grandmothers early in life and multiple close aunts and uncles and some very close friends, it did not compare to losing my beloved husband, Fred. No, this was my first "real" experience into the Tar Pit as well as on the path that led me to it, and I would have to continue to follow the path to get through the Pit.

The reason for the Tart Pit postings on Facebook started as a way to communicate with the masses, but it became cathartic for me. I wrote a great deal in junior high and high school, but mostly short stories and poems. It was comforting and a source of stress relief. I had no time for such things in college. When I graduated, started working full-time, got married, and started raising a family, I put writing and journaling aside. Funny how we tend to return to our roots. My journaling as a much younger version of me was very private; this Facebook posting was so public and felt very uncomfortable. I immediately received feedback from many about how much it was helping them deal with their own Tar Pit experiences, so I continued on with posting my thoughts and feelings.

The path is what I started walking first with Fred and the family, and now we walk it without Fred physically with us. Just like hiking, every hiker has a different perspective and a different interpretation of the view. Over the years of hiking, our family sometimes hiked quietly to absorb the sights and sounds, sometimes we chattered about what we were seeing or smelling or hearing, and sometimes we sang or made up silly jingles as we walked because the hiking was tedious and the view wasn't particularly impressive. Moving along the path has been similar, although certainly not as fun as hiking. Talking about the experience helps at times, and sometimes, quietly moving along has been all the energy I could muster. I am grateful, though, that I seem to be moving along the path through the Tar Pit.

At some point, the path will lead to a road, and hopefully, the road leads to a new journey. I like journeys! Stepping off the path to begin the journey will be fraught with its own issues. There is a saying that "misery loves company." When trudging along the path with fellow "Tar Pit dwellers," there is solace in knowing others feel your pain. It is my hope that, as I step off the path someday and look out onto my new journey, I will continue to offer hope to my fellow Tar Pit dwellers that their journey is ahead of them too.

Shock and Awe, Sadness vs. Anger

Years ago, the Gulf War began, and Operation Desert Shield was initiated from August 1990 to January 1991. It then moved into Operation Desert Storm in January–February 1991. When Desert Storm began, General Schwarzkopf and President H.W. Bush talked about the "shock and awe" of the attack. The premise was, that there would be so many missiles fired on Iraq and the areas of Kuwait invaded by Iraq, that the people in the area, as well as the world, would be filled with "shock and awe." The plan was that the war would basically end before it really got started. I don't know why but that phrase stuck in my mind.

Fast forward to May of 2016. I think most of us know that bad things can happen to anyone at any time. We understand accidents happen, people get very ill, and death occurs. We understand that intellectually as humans, but I think most of us think it won't happen to us or someone close to us. Fred and I weren't much different. I think the difference for Fred was that he had been through his own "shock and awe" when his dad was diagnosed with cancer and subsequently lost his battle in August 1982.

At first, Fred was too confused to understand his diagnosis fully. He did ask me repeatedly during the drive to the James on the first day what was wrong. I told him he had a brain tumor and we were going to the hospital for treatment. He remembered his dad had several surgeries, and he asked when his surgery would be and if it would cure him. I already knew that, based on the size and location of the tumor, there would be no surgery to try to excise the tumor. At best, there would be a biopsy to confirm the diagnosis and get a treatment plan started. I also knew it was doubtful that he would survive, but I did not want to take all hope away from him, or me for that matter. It was just too painful to bear.

My own "shock and awe" actually began the moment I thought "brain tumor" the Wednesday before the MRI. It was sinking in as I watched Fred's condition decline over Mother's Day weekend. Then the shock turned to overwhelming sadness as we drove to the James the day of his diagnosis. Oddly, I didn't experience anger. Fear certainly was in the mix of emotions though.

After Fred's symptoms began to improve with the steroids, we began to talk about our feelings and our lives together up until this point. We both knew we had been blessed to be together for over thirty-two years and married almost thirty-two years. We were so very grateful for two wonderful sons, a terrific family, and a great group of friends. We talked about the many trips we took as a couple and as a family. Such wonderful memories we had been given. Fred and I both had a deep faith in God and believed, and I still do, in the resurrection through Christ Jesus. As we talked, we knew, someday, we would be together in eternity.

We spent a great deal of time praying and crying the night before his surgery and for the next few days before bringing him home. We shared wonderful stories about our marriage with the staff at the James. In fact, they named Fred's room "the crying room" because everyone left Fred's room crying when we shared our stories of love and faithfulness. Even after Fred was discharged, we shared stories with others about how we felt we had been blessed throughout our lives. We also told others that God is good and that no matter how this turned out, we had faith that we would see each other again in heaven. We had the obligatory meetings with the social worker during some of our outpatient visits during chemo and radiation. She finally cancelled the meetings as she felt we were coping well and there wasn't more to be offered because we had such wonderful family and friend support as well as our faith.

Anyone who has studied anything remotely related to healthcare has studied Elizabeth Kubler Ross's stages of grief. One of the stages is anger. It is interesting that I have never felt anger over Fred's diagnosis and death, and as far as I know, Fred was never angry either. He was very sad, though, at the thought of leaving all of us, but he knew he would pass on to heaven. He said he wasn't afraid of dying; he just wasn't ready to leave us yet. It's certain we weren't ready for him to leave us either, but we weren't in denial. The gravity of the situation hit us in the face from day one, and it never went away.

Our hopes and our prayers, as we discussed many times, was that God would cure Fred. Of course, God answers prayers in His own way, and ultimately, Fred was cured when he died and was no longer in pain. We prayed that God's will would be done and that He would give us the strength to walk the path placed before us. We wanted Fred to be cured and for people to say, "Wow, look what great faith can do," or if Fred did not survive, for people to say, "That must be an amazing God that they showed faith even though Fred died." Either way, it was going to be God's will and not ours, and we had to put it in His hands. As a self-proclaimed control freak, putting anything in anyone's hands is a challenge for me. God has a way of bringing us to our knees to depend solely on Him and not on our own resources.

One of the biggest emotions I have dealt with throughout the Tar Pit path is one of profound sadness. Sadness at the loss of what I had planned with my special man (like being with Fred for at least fifty years), sadness that the boys would not watch their dad grow old, sadness that our granddaughter Eva will never know her Papa Schwan except through pictures and shared stories, and our granddaughter Jordyn will barely remember him. I have sadness that Mom (Schwan) Rogers would watch her son die, sadness that Fred's siblings would lose their only brother, and the list goes on. The sadness is deep, dark, and overpowering. It causes the type of pain that nothing can ease. It is a pain that cuts so deeply that, at the time, you feel you never will heal or be whole. Again, God has a way of bringing us to our knees, but when we are there, He begins to heal us and take the pain away. I have been on my knees a great deal! I can honestly say, though, that I have not ever felt anger at anyone, especially God, for Fred's death.

As I have said many, many times, I do feel blessed. I had a really amazing man in my life for over thirty-two years, and we were married for most of that time. We were blessed with wonderful sons, and Fred was able to see both boys married and enjoyed being "Dad Schwan" to Lisa and Michelle. He got to know Jordyn and lived long enough to see Eva be born. We felt that to be angry was to be ungrateful for the blessings we had been given. We just felt sad.

I certainly do not feel that those who go through all the stages of grief, including experiencing anger, are doing it wrong or don't have faith; it just wasn't something that Fred and I did. I think some of our reaction is the amount of pain, suffering, and death that Fred and I saw over the many years in our careers. Fred had forty years in the fire service as dispatcher, volunteer firefighter, full-time firefighter/paramedic, or captain. I had over thirty-five years in nursing in various roles including ICU nursing. We saw people suffer a long time with extended illnesses. We saw families lose a loved one in an instant with no time to prepare, or to say the things that needed to be said, or to plan for the inevitable-death. We were grateful that we had time. We had a chance for a successful treatment with chemo and radiation; however, numbers don't lie, and most people with glioblastoma do not live a long-term life after being diagnosed. Generally, the quality of life after diagnosis for those who do survive is not good. Miracles do happen though, and there have been some amazing success stories.

It may seem odd to feel blessed and feel almost unbearably sad at the same time, and yet that is exactly how the two of us felt. I still feel that way today, although the deep sadness has lifted and isn't as unbearable and suffocating. The sadness comes in waves and pulls me backward and deeper into the Tar Pit, but I can still make forward motion most of the time. I imagine that some of the sadness will always be with me. The loss of my soulmate has forever changed me. I have grown, even through the loss. I still am overwhelmed with "shock and awe." Usually it happens when I least expect it. I am improving though in my reactions, and each day, I think I am moving forward despite the backsliding which I think will always occur.

Things Not to Say to Someone Who Is Grieving

First and foremost, until Fred died, I really don't think I had a clue about the tips I am about to give. As empathetic as we all try to be for our family and friends, until we actually walk in the shoes of those going through grief, we can't possibly know how it feels. While we want to give comfort, we have to recognize there are no perfect words to "fix" the grief. What we think is quite helpful and profound when sharing our thoughts with a grieving person, is most likely not helpful at all.

I can say with certainty that most, if not all, of those grieving are not comforted by comments such as "He/She is in a better place," "God needed another angel so He called your loved one home," "God must have had a reason for wanting your loved one in heaven," or "Time heals all things," etc. I have talked to many people who have been in the Tar Pit about things that aren't helpful to hear when grieving. Almost 100 percent of the time, those statements aren't comforting. Another very common comment is "You need to be happy and focus on the positive." This comment certainly does more harm than good to the grieving person's emotional well-being, and it minimizes the depth of the pain the person is experiencing. Finally, "Make sure you take care of yourself" might as well be "You need to run a marathon and hike a mountain" to a grieving person. If those in the Tar Pit had it all figured out regarding taking care of themselves, they most likely wouldn't be floundering in the pit.

A majority of the time, when a grieving person is venting and sharing thoughts and feelings, that person is not looking for advice or words of wisdom. Nothing can be said to bring the loved one back, and that is really the only thing the grieving person wants. Pit dwellers do not expect those around them to fix anything and make it better. Albeit, we wish someone could magically make the pain go away, but we know that isn't possible. I have found the biggest thing I have wanted and needed, other than having Fred back alive, was just having someone listen to me and be present with me, though sometimes I needed—and still do—my solitude.

People often feel compelled to say something when a person is grieving; however, just sitting quietly actually "speaks volumes." The quiet presence of sitting with another human being when his or her heart is breaking is a wonderful gift, but it is difficult for most people to do. We somehow feel that we have to be saying "comforting things." It is difficult to see someone grieving and in emotional pain, and most of us have not been trained in grief counseling.

One of the most therapeutic statements people have made to me is this: "Karin, I don't know what to say other than I am sorry for your loss." I always tell people that I appreciate their honesty. I am comforted that the person isn't trying to come up with some type of trite comment, which wasn't going to make me feel better. I often tell people I don't know what to say either. I also do not sugarcoat the situation. I tell others it was awful, devastating. and horrible. I follow that statement up with, "But God is good, and I am blessed that we all shared Fred for his time on earth. I am doing better than I was a year ago."

The bottom line is that we are all born and we all die. It is the fact of life. When we try to come up with a perfect comment to somehow make it all better, less painful, more meaningful, etc., we minimize the fact that the death of a loved one is incredibly painful and words cannot make it better. I wish I could write that, as time has gone by, it wasn't as bad as I thought it was at the time I was going through it. I can't do that though. The feeling of being sucker-punched repeatedly, and the "foggy feeling" of continuing to walk in a terrible nightmare, is still very real to me. I will say though that, in time, the sharpness of the experience has dulled. While I remember all those feelings, I do not feel them as acutely as I did throughout 2016 after Fred's diagnosis and death. In that respect, time has begun to heal the deep wounds.

I have found that, over the years, people have felt I was "strong." I don't know if that is good or bad or exactly how that happened. I can tell you I certainly did not feel strong throughout the process of Fred's diagnosis and subsequent death. In fact, I felt very weak and vulnerable while walking the path through the Tar Pit. Telling me that I am strong and "time heals all things" was not comforting. It actually made me feel worse because I felt I that I could not live up to other's expectations. I wanted to simply break and felt I couldn't, but maybe, just maybe, that was a good thing.

If I had only me to think about it would have been so easy to give up. I have tendencies toward being hermit-like, and if I had to be only concerned about my own well-being after Fred died, I would have rolled up my mat, tucked in the edges, and rotted from the inside out. That would have been incredibly selfish of me and certainly wouldn't have helped those I loved as they too walked their Tar Pit path. For you see, I wasn't the only one who lost Fred on September 22, 2016. We had two sons who lost their dad, a mother who lost her only son, sisters who lost their only brother, my parents who lost their son-in-law, three brothers-in-law and a sister-in-law who lost their beloved Fred, and countless nieces/nephews/cousins who were also grieving. Let's not forget the two little girls who Papa Schwan would not see dance at their weddings someday. Not to mention, the community lost a wonderful man who gave freely of his time, talent, and money. For me to be so self-absorbed that I could not be strong for all of these people who had been my rock and strength would have been ungrateful of me.

I share all of this so that those who are walking in the Tar Pit know they are not alone in their struggle to not give up and throw in the towel. I also share this so that those standing on the edge cheering the Tar Pit dwellers on to the shore understand that trite comments don't help, but your presence does. Your understanding, and sometimes just your quiet presence, are exactly what we need. Do not give up on us; we truly are trudging along as fast as we can in our continuously exhausted state.

I look back now with a completely different perspective on what I can do to be a lighthouse to others walking on the path through the Tar Pit. Throughout my career, I have sat, stood, and cried with many families who have faced the death of a loved one. While it has been difficult, I also believe it was a gift. I found several times that the families seemed to comfort me more than I did them because the loss was emotional for me as well as for the family. (Actually, that is empathizing just a little too much with the family.) Learning to be a quiet but strong presence to those grieving does not come easy. It isn't a situation that most of us face on a regular basis. How can we possibly be "good" at something that is so incredibly uncomfortable to watch and experience?

Simply saying "I am sorry" and then quietly pausing truly is the best gift we can give a grieving person. Taking the cue from that person as to whether he or she needs a hug, a pat on the back, or completely left alone is the next step. Just a hint: the grieving person often doesn't know what he or she wants either. I tend to like hugs, or sometimes I just don't want touched at all. I laugh and say that I am like a cat; either I want to sit on your lap or I don't want to even be in the same room with you.

Patience and presence are two wonderful gifts you can give to the grieving person. As he or she experiences "cat-like" moments, understanding and adapting will go a long way to support those grieving. Your understanding and flexibility help tremendously as the grieving person musters the energy to keep moving forward on the path through the Tar Pit.

Sainthood and the Peanut Butter Spoon

How in the world, you might ask, can grief, sainthood, and a peanut butter spoon all end up in the same sentence, let alone in the same paragraph and frame of thought? It's quite simple really, when you understand how the threads weave through the story.

I think many of us have the tendency to only think of the positive qualities of our loved ones after they have died. It seems sacrilegious to think of, let alone dwell on, anything negative or less than complimentary about our loved one. After all, they are not here to defend themselves from anything negative we might think or dare say out loud. As time goes by, we focus more and more on the positive attributes, and those become bigger than life. Our loved one takes on additional positive qualities the more we think about them, and we actually lose focus on reality. Before we know it, we have bestowed sainthood on our loved one.

The sainthood phenomenon isn't really fair to our loved one or to ourselves and can be dangerously detrimental to our ability to adequately grieve and move through the Tar Pit. If we see our loved one as perfect, or nearly so, then the anger we feel for our loss, as well the undone projects or the pile of papers left on the desk or the tools spread all over the shop (hopefully you are getting the message), seem wrong, and we feel guilty. While wallowing in the Tar Pit and treading thick tar, one of the last things we need is to also wallow in guilt.

I knew Fred was really a wonderful man. He was a great friend, husband, father, son, brother, uncle, and the perfect match for me. As more and more people heard of his diagnosis and struggle with cancer, I heard from many people regarding their fond memories of him. I didn't know Fred as a child or young man, so I could only go on the stories people willingly shared with me. The stories were funny, sweet, heartfelt, and always positive.

The boys and I frequently shared stories about Fred as we kept the bedside vigil and we continue to share stories about him well after his death. We laughed about so many memories. Fred was a funny man; sometimes he wasn't trying to be funny, but he seemed to always make us laugh. At times, I laughed at him out of shear exasperation in our over thirty-two years together!

As stories are shared and retold, they take on a bigger than life perspective. It is easy to go down the path of thinking of our loved one as a saint, someone who did not have character flaws or imperfections. However, the character flaws often made our loved one so endearing to us. By assigning saint status, we change who they were, and our relationship with them changes as well.

I often said that I was the only woman who could have been married to Fred for thirty-two years. He was frustrating at times, imperfect, and exasperating. At the same time, he was loveable, dedicated, supportive, and nurturing, He was the perfect man for me to raise sons with and begin to grow old with as well. What I also know is that he was the only man who could have gone through everything with me that he did and still stay married to me. I think I got the better side of the deal between the two of us.

So how does this all lead to a peanut butter spoon? Anyone who has been in a long-term relationship knows that our partner will do things that make us annoyed, irritated, or generally drive us crazy. Fred and I were no different. I think I probably did more things that drove him crazy than he did to me. Generally, he kept quiet (to me) or mumbled just enough that I couldn't understand what he was saying. There was one thing that he was quite verbal about though. He could not understand how I could leave peanut butter on a spoon after I licked it.

I am a vegetarian and often have a spoon of peanut butter in the morning as part of my breakfast or throughout the day as a snack. I eat the peanut butter off the spoon and lay it down in the sink. I do not lick it perfectly clean. Since I do not have a dishwasher other than the two hands attached to my arms, I lay the spoon in the sink until I do the dishes the next time.

For some reason, a spoon with a little bit of peanut butter still left on it drove Fred crazy. He would not mumble about it; instead, he would grumble about it, often loudly, and rarely would it be a short grumble. Even after his diagnosis with brain cancer, he focused on the peanut butter spoon and maybe more so than before the diagnosis. As long as he was able to do so, he would do the dishes in the morning as I finished getting ready for work to help me out with my additional responsibilities. As he scrubbed the peanut butter off the spoon, he would comment about how he didn't understand how I could leave perfectly good peanut butter on the spoon.

The period of time from Fred's diagnosis through his death was intense and overwhelming, I didn't have time to ponder the peanut butter spoon. I will never forget, though, the first time I laid the spoon in the sink after Fred died. It took my breath away; all those times flashed back on me: years of me leaving the spoon in the sink, years of him grumbling, far too few months of him scrubbing the spoon as I got ready for work.

I realized that Fred's grumbling about the spoon annoyed me as much as the peanut butter on the spoon annoyed him. I also realized our marriage wasn't perfect, though it was pretty darn good. I reflected that he wasn't perfect or a saint and that I wasn't perfect either, but it was our imperfections that made us so good together.

I still eat my peanut butter off the spoon, and I still lay it in the sink until I do the dishes. I smile now and think of Fred not as a saint but as a human with strengths, weaknesses, and flaws, which made me love him so very much. I think he looks down and grumbles sometimes when he sees the spoon, but I also think he smiles when he sees it as well. That is what helps me continue to take forward steps through the Tar Pit.

The Valley Experience

From almost the moment Fred and I met, we clicked with many of the things we liked to do. We both loved the outdoors and traveling, so our honeymoon was spent hiking around Mammoth Cave in Kentucky. We spent vacations doing exciting activities such as white-water rafting, hiking up into the mountains in Glacier National Park or Acadia National Park, and hiking down to the bottom of the Grand Canyon and back out. We also did several safaris in Africa, hiked to the top of the Sydney Harbor Bridge in Australia, visited Disney World, went on mission trips, and camped. I am really quite amazed at how much we packed into thirty-two years together when I sit back and reflect or reminisce as I go through photo albums.

One hike Fred never did with me was in Yosemite National Park. I had the opportunity to hike the park several times with Nicolaus, but the timing for having Tioga Pass open when Fred visited that area with me never allowed for us to have the road open. I always wanted him to hike Yosemite with me as the contrasts of the mountains and rocks with the deep valleys are simply stunning. We would have had so much fun hiking, talking about the beautiful scenery, and whining about how sore we were the next day after all the hiking.

My favorite hike in Yosemite is along the Tuolumne River and the hike that goes to Glen Aulin. The hike starts in the Tuolumne Meadows and follows the huge rock formations until coming out at the quiet and calm part of the river. It quickly loses altitude and the river becomes a rushing series of rapids and calm and then rapids again with stunning views at every turn. I enjoyed stopping along the way to see the mountains in the distance, listening to the rush of the rapids near me, and looking forward to what is around the bend.

The whole time I was descending lower and lower, and the views continued to be more majestic at each turn.

The contrast of Yosemite reminds me a great deal of life with mountain and valley experiences. I never was particularly drawn to Psalm 23. Don't get me wrong, it isn't that I don't like Psalm 23, it just never "spoke" to me. I know that many people have it either read at their funerals or included on the memory card for calling hours. My maternal grandmother had it read at her funeral. I was young when she died, and I have missed her so much; I think I developed a bit of an aversion to it. For whatever reason, though, I decided it would not be part of Fred's funeral, and I didn't think I wanted it for mine either.

I attend church generally on Saturday nights, and I frequently am awake early on Sunday mornings, so for several years now, I have watched Charles Stanley on Sunday mornings. I have found him to be consistent and very scripturally based. It is interesting how many times Charles Stanley's message coincides or compliments the pastor's sermon on Saturday night. It really is uncanny at times. It is almost as if God gives me the initial message on Saturday and reinforces it on Sunday morning.

Recently, Pastor Riesen, the senior pastor at Trinity Lutheran Church where I have been a lifelong member, preached on Psalm 23 and explained it in a way that I had not heard previously. He explained that the "valley experience" is that deep experience when we are at a low point; it may be related to something that has happened in a relationship or job loss, death of a family member or friend, or may be as we face death ourselves. It is a low point and certainly could be a point when we feel most distant from God and incredibly alone and frightened. According to Charles Stanley, valley experiences are most profitable for learning when we feel loneliness, and so we turn to God. We tend to learn the most about God in our valley experiences where we rest, we drink, and we allow God's rod and staff (the Bible) to comfort and protect us.

That imagery totally changes Psalm 23 for me. I always envisioned that it was about laying down in cool green grass and just resting. I tend to be an overscheduled type of person, so the thought of just lying around in cool green grass really didn't conjure up peace and solitude for me. Now I understand it! I "get" that the valley experience is where we are when we are in grief, feeling lost, and feeling pain filled. It is then that we need to stop and allow God to sustain us through His word and guidance. It is the valley experience that allows us to hear the still small voice guiding our next steps. Oh, how I have needed to hear that voice on a regular basis, particularly on those days when I feel so incredibly lost and my heart aches. While the depth and length of the valley experience depends on our response to the experience, it is actually preparing us for the next mountain experience to follow.

The "mountain experience" is what most of us probably long for the most. Being on top of a mountain is exhilarating, particularly when we have climbed the mountain. My birthday is in July, and one year, there was a church bus trip to the Smoky Mountains which coincided with my birthday. Fred was unable to come with the boys and me. He wanted us to go, and never being one to turn down an adventure, I headed off on the trip with Nicolaus and Christopher. We hiked a path along a river and then we hiked up to one of the domes of rocks; it was spectacular sitting on the rocks with our sons, but Fred was painfully absent. I missed him so much.

I reflect back on that trip and realize that, though I was physically at the top of the rock, I think that was a precursor to a "valley experience." What should have been exhilarating wasn't quite what I thought it would be since Fred wasn't there to share it with us. Fred's diagnosis and battle with brain cancer was probably the most difficult "valley experience" I have ever had; I know I will have more though however. I honestly don't want any more of those kinds of experiences, but we humans are prone to those; it's part of the human existence.

I have had many "mountain experiences," the joy of becoming a parent, the awesomeness of seeing a grandchild born, the grace we are given from others when we don't deserve it, the thought of salvation from an awesome God who loves us despite the fact we sin every day. Then there are the physical "mountain experiences" of watching a sunset on Cadillac Mountain in Acadia National Park,

KARIN SCHWAN

of standing on Tabletop Mountain in Capetown, South Africa, of watching Nicolaus stand above me on Lambert Dome in Yosemite National Park, or watching Christopher get off the troop bus on his safe return from Afghanistan.

Before Christopher deployed, Fred and I decided we wanted to have a special family trip. We knew in the back of our minds that Christopher may not return to us, and we wanted something special to remember and help sustain us. All five of us—Nicolaus, Lisa, Christopher, Fred and I—decided that Hawaii would be our destination, and we picked Maui as our home base. We took a day trip to Oahu to tour the island, specifically Pearl Harbor. As usual, the kids thought I overscheduled the trip, but we saw many things, snorkeled in the ocean several times, went on whale watching trips, went to a luau, and went to Haleakala National Park. We arose very early and were picked up for a trip to the top of the mountain in the dark so we would be in place for the sunrise. Even though my family didn't embrace the thought of the middle of the night "mountain experience," they begrudgingly got up, waited for the van to pick us up, whined a little, and slept on the way to the top. Once we were in place, standing in the dark and the cold, we began to see the tip of the sunrise over the horizon. All the lack of sleep and feeling cold were worth the spectacular sight we witnessed. And while we enjoyed the experience, we knew we couldn't stay at the top; we had to come down. That experience is still the one we talk about as a very special time. The kids also laugh at their "overscheduling mom" who always thinks she can do more in less time than is humanly possible.

What I have learned through my Tar Pit path is that if I hadn't had the "valley experiences" and have the foundation that God would sustain me through them, I think I wouldn't appreciate the "mountain experiences" as much. We need to have contrasts in our lives. We need to understand that we cannot depend on ourselves to climb out of the valley and ascend the mountain. We also need to understand that we can't live at the top of the mountain all the time. The air is thin, the resources are few, and the emotion is too intense to stay at the top of the mountain all the time. We have to make the descent, and sometimes, we have to dwell in the valley and allow God's rod and staff to comfort us.

Joining "the Club"

Before Fred's diagnosis, I had many friends and family members who had loved ones die. I honestly felt sympathy for them and tried to be supportive and caring. It is different though when you join "the club." This isn't a club anyone wants to join but the loss of a loved one quickly adds the survivor's name to the club roster.

It was uncanny, from 2012 to 2016, how many of my coworkers had spouses die or they died themselves. Many of them died of cancer, and more than I would have expected had brain cancer. I attended as many funerals as I could, sent sympathy cards, and donated money to memorial funds. I remember thinking, *Boy, I don't know how I could get through the loss of Fred*. Little did I know that every funeral I attended and every discussion I had with a survivor was training for what I would experience in 2016.

While I tried to be understanding when the survivor seemed "in a fog" or "unmotivated," it was sometimes frustrating when I needed that person to be productive at work or needed them to be more responsive to my communications with them. I would like to think I wasn't insensitive about it, but I can't guarantee that I was always as understanding as I could have or should have been. People gave me grace though, and I never had anyone call me out for being inconsiderate, so I hope I was more supportive and caring than not.

Once Fred was diagnosed and then died, I had a new understanding and appreciation of how the deep and painful loss of a spouse feels. I know the loss of a child must be deeply painful as well; however, I cannot begin to try and say I know how a parent feels when they lose a child. I did see the pain very keenly in Mom Rogers and that was on the heels of losing Dad Rogers and then Dad Schwan years before that. I simply do not know how she managed being in two "clubs," that of surviving a spouse, twice, and that of surviving a child.

I never would have asked to be a member of the "surviving spouse club." While I felt that I would certainly outlive Fred because of our age difference and that fact he was the male, I did not imagine that, at age fifty-five, I would be a widow. As I have said before, I envisioned that we would be married at least fifty years, so I "planned" on him living into his eighties. Being a widow in my seventies was what I expected. Life certainly has a way of not going according to our plans.

When I was young, I was a member of 4-H, Brownies and then Girl Scouts, the Young Scientists Club, FHA, etc. I was used to being in clubs and organizations. When joining a club or organization, we are generally indoctrinated by those already in the club so we know how to behave. We learn from other members how to perform to be successful and what we will learn by being a member in the club. I hope I do not offend anyone reading this, but I named my "club" the "Dead Spouse Club." The name is not intended to make light of the seriousness of the situation; it is blunt and raw, exactly how I felt when I joined "the club."

I had many people reach out to me with love and support after Fred died. I had people give me tips about how to deal with the pain and the grief. The truth of the matter is, though, each loss is very personal, and it is difficult to indoctrinate others as they enter "the club." While we are members with many in the club, we also are all on our own at the same time. I remember pulling into the drive by myself after Fred's funeral. I had all the pictures and mementoes packed in my car. I sat there and realized I had to unpack all of it myself, put it all away, and that wherever I left things in the house, that is where they would stay because only I lived in the house now. It isn't that I didn't realize I was by myself prior to that; however, the stark reality of being in the Dead Spouse Club hit me incredibly hard at that moment. It was all I could do to get out of the car and walk into the house. It felt different that day, and it is difficult to explain, but I have had discussions with others who have had similar experiences. I am grateful that I came home by myself, though, because I got through the initial shock of being by myself. If one of my sons, my parents, or someone else would have been with me, I would have had to face it eventually anyway. It was nice to have that initial shock behind me.

Now when I know someone who has lost a spouse, I try to reach out prior to the funeral and check on how that person is doing. I might call or text if I know the person well, or I may write a note in the sympathy card. I don't pontificate about loss and grief, but I let the person know that this is difficult and painful, that they will feel weak and everyone will tell them they are strong. I let them know they will feel like they can't get through it but…they will be stronger than they think, and they will indeed survive the funeral. I write in the note or tell them that the loneliness will hit them when they walk into their house after the funeral. I generally include my phone number in the card and ask the person to call me if they need to talk, need someone to sit with them, or if there is anything I can do for them.

I don't have all the answers, and I still struggle some days more than others in walking through the Tar Pit. I do not pretend to be an expert on grief. I do feel I am an expert on *my* grief and Tar Pit dwelling though. Most days, I feel a twinge of loneliness, and some days, it stings much more. Most days I do not cry, but some days, I cry multiple times. I can say that, in a very odd way, I feel blessed that I understand the Dead Spouse Club and can hopefully offer comfort and support to those who join the club. I don't know why God decided that Fred should be called to heaven in September of 2016. I do feel it is God's will that those of us who are members of the club should help indoctrinate new members and hold them up as they work to gain their footing their own Tar Pit. As we extend a hand to that person, we become a strong link for them. We are stronger when we are giving of ourselves and reaching out to others through our grief. We Tar Pit dwellers can help to give meaning to the loss we are experiencing by helping others.

About a year after Fred died, a friend stopped to ask how I was doing. He had joined the Dead Spouse Club about nine years ahead of me. I was coming up on the end of the first year, and he was coming up on ten years. It was as if a floodgate opened, and I had a fellow club member to talk to and ask questions that I hadn't asked others. He had survived all the "firsts" and many other life events, and I wanted his knowledge and support. He patiently listened as I dumped almost a year of pent-up questions. I spoke of wanting to hurry through the grief process and get to the shore of the Tar Pit. His comment to me was, "Karin, it's been ten years for me. You need to give yourself time. You can't rush through it."

I admit that his words of wisdom weren't exactly what I wanted to hear at the time, but it was sage advice. I think of that conversation often when I get impatient with myself. I sit back and think, *Am I further ahead today than I was a year ago?* Almost always, I can answer that question with a resounding yes. Club membership isn't voluntary. We go kicking and screaming into this club, but once we become members, we can reach out to others as they enter the club and offer sound advice and support.

I have connected with so many of my patients over the past two years since Fred's diagnosis and subsequent death. We seem to all have "the look" in our eyes. So many struggle with the loneliness and grief which subsequently spills into our well-being and health. As I talk to people and get a feeling about their sense of humor and ability to handle mine, I often tell people, "Ye who dies first wins." At first, I think this takes people aback, but then a smile almost always comes. I talk about all of my "stuff" and how now I am left with all of "Fred's stuff." He got to enjoy his "stuff" without the burden of sorting it or throwing it away. I tell people that there will be a serious discussion with him once I get to heaven and he is waiting for me across the thin veil separating us.

I Feel Crazy... What Do I Do with All This Stuff?

First, I want to say that I do not use the word "crazy" in a mean, inflammatory or derogatory way. In this world of always being "PC," or politically correct, I realize calling someone crazy can seem insensitive. I have a deep respect for mental health issues, and in no way am I making light of that. The "crazy" I refer to is that feeling most of us have had when overwhelmed, unable to make a simple decision, and can't figure out what we need to do next all bundled into one all-consuming feeling. If you have been able to escape that kind of feeling in your life, I am impressed. I am not sure I would refer to it as being lucky though. For me, getting to that point of "crazy" has certainly allowed me to be more vulnerable and rawer, as well as more honest with others walking in their own Tar Pits.

I have a friend who lost her husband to cancer one month after I lost Fred. My friend's husband had a much longer cancer battle than did Fred, but both men valiantly tried to defeat it. In the end, cancer won the first round, but they ultimately won because they are both in heaven with God, and that is a true victory.

I see my friend most weeks at church. We do a check-in of sorts to see how we are doing, and all we have to do is look at one another, and we understand the look that a fellow Tar Pit dweller gives to another. Some weeks, we talk about what is going on in our lives, and some weeks, we just hug; it may be too painful to discuss, we just know what the other is going through.

One week, my friend asked me if I felt like I was going crazy. I laughed and told her that I was a little that way before Fred's diagnosis, but I certainly struggle with "my crazy" on a daily basis. I cannot understand how I can go from laughing and smiling to sobbing uncontrollably to pulling it all together with my "public on-stage" persona in a relatively short period of time. I suppose there is something pathological about that in itself, but I figure it is just the way it is, and I need to accept it.

I heard someone refer to the "craziness" as "widow's brain," and I think I agree. Of course, it could be "widower's brain" or simply "survivor's brain." I used to be a fairly capable organizer and planner. I always had a plan A, plan B, and sometimes a plan C. I think it came from years of nursing, where the patient rarely was textbook in presentation or response to therapy and being prepared was vital to keeping my patients alive on ICU. I now have a difficult time even spelling plan A, let alone having one, and plan B and C seem to escape me most days. Trying to get organized and then stay organized is such an overwhelming task at times that I simply drop what I am doing and walk away. That is extremely uncharacteristic of me.

There are times when I seem to pull it all together and get my game plan organized, implement the plan, and pull it off almost flawlessly. I relish in those moments because I feel like "me" again. The truth of the matter, though, is that I had frequent times of not being able to pull off my game plan before the Tar Pit. I think I just don't feel the resilience I used to, and my tolerance is less for feeling incomplete or inept. I have always been a perfectionist and hard on myself, so I am not sure who I am kidding about tolerance.

I am learning I have to give myself the grace to laugh, cry, laugh, and sob in a relatively short period of time. I need to understand that I may be excited one minute about going somewhere I have been looking forward to only to change my mind at the last minute because life is just too complex at that moment, and I cancel my plans. I am sure this is annoying to many people who are used to me following through regardless, and I would not have understood it until I experienced it myself. If you know people struggling with this type of on again/off again plan making, please give them grace. If you are struggling with it, give yourself grace; it does get better over time.

I think part of my feeling of being overwhelmed and "crazy" is based on the plans I had for my future and what I envisioned it would look like with Fred in it. Proof once again that we have little control over anything more than a moment in time and our reaction to the moment. Ah…the "living in the moment" mantra so many of us espouse but so few of us really master.

I have said for years, and I really do believe it, that we are all neurotic, and quirky and "normal" doesn't exist. Some people channel their neurotic tendencies to their benefit in such ways as using being obsessive-compulsive to being a good organizer and following through. Some people channel their addictive personality traits to focusing on exercising vs. consuming illegal drugs or large quantities of alcohol. I think if we are honest with ourselves, we all struggle with channeling our inner quirkiness to something we can reveal to others and not be labeled as "crazy."

When we grow together with someone, like a spouse, we learn we can reveal many of our inner quirkiness to that person and he or she loves us because of, and in spite of, the quirks. Sometimes, those become our most endearing qualities. When we lose our trusted loved one, the fear of being exposed to others with our frailties and oddities makes us feel even more broken, and thus, the "craziness" of the self-doubt either begins or, for most of us, worsens.

I haven't discovered how to fix the issue of the self-doubt: the worry that I am too quirky for others to accept, that I am too broken to piece back together into something that resembles me again, that if others see my "crazy" of indecisiveness and insecurity, they will think I am a fraud, and that list goes on. I think I am recognizing that only my trust in God can "fix" me though. All the self-help and self-reflection books in the word will never stand up to the Great Physician.

It's incredibly humbling realizing that, when you are used to seeing yourself as "the" person who is supposed to fix things and can't, you have to accept help. There is a time to step back and get down on your knees and pray for healing. This is the time for allowing God to take the lead. As I have worked to change my approach to the crazy times in the Tar Pit, I have found the bowing down before God has been the best approach yet.

For me, part of "the crazy" is looking around my house and property and seeing over thirty-two years of a life together and trying to sort out what goes and what stays. I think it is safe to say that most of us have too much "stuff." I can say for certainty that Fred and I certainly had way too much stuff. I jokingly have said, though in all seriousness too, that "the first one who dies wins." Fred left me all his "treasures" as well as all of my own. I am not talking about the usual things we leave behind like clothes, shoes, and a few collectables. Oh no, I am talking about hundreds of hats, enough fire memorabilia to open a fire history museum, and a plethora of nuts/bolts/screws. I have more than enough "pieces parts" of equipment, partially used notepads, pens, and the list goes on and on, that I could open my own flea market.

At times, I feel full of energy and fully intend to begin cleaning out the nooks and crannies holding Fred's "stuff." I was pretty quick in dealing with his clothes, shoes/boots, coats, and the *many* hats. I felt if I at least whittled those down, I would feel like I was making a forward step through the Tar Pit. I do feel it was therapeutic. To see all his clothes, and especially his hats, sitting around or hanging in the closet for months would have been so painful. I did keep some of his clothes for some special projects and a few shirts to sleep in. I wear some of his hats when I am outside working.

For some reason, I am having a more difficult time with the "stuff." In fact, I still have an entire tray full of keys sitting on a table in my kitchen. I have no idea what those keys go to and probably never will, and yet I can't seem to get rid of them. It serves no purpose to keep them, but there is an odd sense of finality in getting rid of them, so they still take up space on my table.

I wish I could share a wonderful technique that I have learned to deal with "the stuff," but I can't. I think I will struggle with this the rest of my life. Each time I think I have the mental strength and time to sort through things, I find something that I wasn't expecting and I have to walk away in tears. This in turn brings back "the crazy" feeling because I thought I was doing pretty well trudging through the Tar Pit.

It brings me back to the realization that I can't possibly get through the Tar Pit without the strength and guidance of God. He is *the* one who can give us the strength we need to continue in the darkness as we face walking the path through our own Tar Pits.

Ye Who Dies First Wins

I hope that those who have read my writings have been able to understand that despite great loss and pain, I still find a sense of humor to be extremely important. One thing that quickly drew me to Fred was his quick wit and sense of humor. He was able to keep me from taking myself too seriously, or if I did, he quickly would turn it around. One of Fred's endearing qualities was to not take himself too seriously—his ability to stay humble and laugh at himself when he did goofy things. We both were quite capable of "entertaining" each other with some of the dumb things we did.

Fred and I both are (were) collectors. My children think I am a bit of a hoarder. I do really enjoy throwing unneeded things away and being organized; however, my problem stems from not being able to clearly discern what is unneeded. As a nurse, I quickly learned that being able to jerry rig and improvise was important, and in order to improvise, I needed "stuff." The stuff collecting has definitely spilled over into my personal life as well. Having said that, Fred and I amassed quite a collection of stuff in our over thirty-two years of life together as well as our pre-marriage days.

In addition to stuff around the house, shop, and garage, Fred was well known for putting his stuff into bags and boxes with items that clearly were trash: empty Diet Coke bottles, potato chip bags, Snickers wrappers, etc. However, important papers, small items such as nuts/bolts/screws, and loose change with the random dollar bill also found their way into the same bags and boxes. Purging around the house, shop, and garage has been a challenge

As I work to declutter, I feel as if I am geocaching as I go through Fred's "stuff." I can't just look in the bag, see trash, and throw out the bag. I have found things that have made me laugh aloud such as dried fudge in containers or a secret stash of tortilla chips in the same bag as important papers. The things that quickly bring me to tears are poems or letters in Fred's handwriting. When I find anything handwritten, it stops me in my tracks and usually stops my forward progress in cleaning and sorting. Some days, what I find as I am cleaning and sorting is powerful enough that it stops my forward progress in the Tar Pit as well.

When I talk to my fellow Tar Pit dwellers about loss, pain, and healing, we often get to the subject of the stuff our loved ones left behind. There often is a smile that comes over the other person's face, and I almost always say, "Ye who dies first wins." Usually the one I am talking to looks puzzled at first but breaks into a huge smile when I further explain. "The winner" is dubbed when parents, siblings, and other close people in our lives die, but what I feel most closely related to is the death of a spouse. When Fred died, I inherited all of his stuff. We had little time to get everything in order from his diagnosis in May to his death in September 2016, between the shock of the diagnosis, the surgeries, the chemo and radiation, my job, spending time with beloved family and friends, etc. Sorting through stuff was not a priority. As I now climb toward the shore of the Tar Pit and find the energy to actively sort, I am also finding stuff from Fred's dad as well as his mom's stuff. Some things I knew existed, and Fred's plan was to get to them someday, but I have found quite a few things which I did not know were here.

In the end, I am left literally holding the bags and boxes of stuff. I am fully aware that things, stuff, and worldly possessions mean very little. However, for me, they represent so much more than their monetary value. Mementos and trinkets evoke memories and often strong emotions as I recall who I was with and what I was doing when those mementos were obtained. Add to the fact that my sons did not get to meet their Grandpa Schwan and thus some of his things like a pocket watch, a model bulldozer, and special rocks he found while excavating may be some of the few links they have to him. The mementoes from England of Mom Schwan Rogers may be the very things that trigger wonderful childhood memories for the boys. The plastic firetrucks and goofy keychains may be something I use to tell our grandchildren what a special man their Papa Schwan was and how he loved them. It isn't easy sorting through "the stuff." It is even harder getting rid of it if it is attached to memories.

I think I may be more a hoarder of memories, and it is manifested in holding onto "stuff." I have rocks, pebbles, shells, and pieces of driftwood that Fred and I collected on our many trips together. None of those items have any monetary value, but the memories of sights, sounds, and smells they evoke are priceless. Each time I think I am going to throw them away, I just can't bring myself to do it. And yet, I know at some point my children and grandchildren will end up going through these "treasured" containers of stuff and wonder why this goofy lady kept pebbles, shells, pieces of driftwood, and rocks. I should get rid of these items before they have to do so; I just can't bring myself to do it yet.

When we die, my faith shows me that we go to heaven to be with our Lord and the stuff of this world is meaningless. The Bible tells us not to store up treasures on earth, and I understand the concept. I fully believe that material possessions do not mean more than people and relationships. I do find these things help with the memories.

While Fred was alive, we were constantly making new memories. Life was full, and yes, we certainly had difficult times, but we had many amazing experiences which have left me with great memories. As I learn my "new normal" life without Fred, I find I miss making new memories with him. I realize that all I have now are the old memories of time with him. It's a stark reality that I do not like. I know it is the reality of my life, but that doesn't mean I like it. Acceptance is a difficult pill to swallow.

As sad as looking back on the memories can be, they also bring me joy and make me smile. I feel the yin and the yang daily. Most days, I can laugh and I still have my sense of humor. When I am dealing with something needing repaired around the house or trying to purge stuff or doing chores Fred used to do, I often talk out loud and tell him "he won." He is in an amazing place, perfectly designed by God, and all the treasures of this life are meaningless. In the meantime, I am left to sort, purge, remember and, yes, smile and cry. Ye who dies first really does win.

In the end, I am happy for Fred. Life means we are born and we die. That is reality. I cannot imagine Fred dealing with all "the stuff" and grief if I had died first, so I am glad he won. However, I would like to discuss the potato chip bags and Snickers wrappers with him, though, as he waits for me when I cross the thin veil someday. And while it won't be the first thing on my list, it may be in my top ten. Well, maybe top twenty.

The Yin and the Yang

Have you ever looked at one of the special pictures that has a variety of images within it, like an old woman and a young lady, or multiple faces? The point is to see what image the viewer sees first. Then there are the famous ink blot tests when the viewer is asked what he or she sees when looking at a black and white image. Most of us also have been asked the question whether "the glass is half empty or half full." The point of all of the observations is to see what the viewer can see first and not what he or she can see all at the same time. From the time we are young, we are taught to make choices; we choose selection A or selection B. While we may want both, we generally are required to choose one.

While I was born in the 1960s, my formative years were in the 1970s. I remember a song with the title "Tears of a Clown" sung by the Miracles. It was a catchy song, but honestly, at the time, I really didn't understand the song even though I sang the words. As I have walked the path through the Tar Pit I have thought about that song and now I understand it. The song was about the loss of a lover and how the singer of the song is smiling on the outside but crying on the inside. He had his game face on for the public but was suffering on the inside.

Until Fred died, I did not understand the deep, dark, and painful side of grief like I do now. Certainly, I had suffered losses and knew sadness, but the kind of loss that I feel without Fred is more painful than anything I could have imagined. Oddly, though, the joy I feel when I look at my sons and their wives and my granddaughters when we are together is incredible. I feel happy yet sad, or maybe it's sad but happy at the same time.

The yin and the yang symbol stands for "dark-bright" or "negative-positive" in Chinese philosophy. It describes the duality that exists in the world of seemingly opposite forces which may actually be complimentary and work together. The philosophy involved in yin-yang is that both forces are needed in the world for balance; one cannot exist without the other. In fact, having one side completely unopposed leads to unbalance. At any given time, though, one force may pull more strongly but both are needed to return to balance.

Our bodies are comprised of forces which need balance. For example, our nervous system has the sympathetic and the parasympathetic nervous systems. The sympathetic nervous system is the "fight or flight" side, and the parasympathetic nervous system is the "feed and breed" side. One cannot go unopposed or we would simply cease to exist. Things can get out of balance; the heart can go too fast or too slow and treatment is needed. The thyroid gland is another example of balance needed within the body. We need a certain amount of thyroid hormone in our bodies, and too much produced by the thyroid gland causes problems; however, too little hormone causes problems as well. Life is about balance.

Being happy all the time sounds wonderful. Having the sunshine and having the weather be perfect everyday sounds, well... perfect. The reality is that if the sun were to shine every day, plants would die; they need rain. We need the dark to complete our circadian rhythm. If we didn't know how it felt to be sad and cry, we would not be able to experience joy and happiness. If we did not experience pain, we would not be able to appreciate being pain-free.

I have to be honest; I hate the fact that I became a widow at age fifty-five and that I have experienced the deep pain of loss. The oddly strange balance to this though is that, because I had the joy of a wonderful marriage with a really terrific partner, I now feel the pain of the loss. If I had never met Fred and had not had over thirty-two years with him, I wouldn't feel the loss. I had to have the light with the dark, the joy with the sadness, the yin with the yang.

I am repeatedly reminded when I read the Bible that God did not promise an easy or happy life, or a life filled with joy. Jesus did not preach that we would not have heartache; He spoke of loving our neighbor, of knowing His followers would be persecuted, of living for our eternal life, not necessarily our worldly life.

As I learn to live with and through my grief, I am also learning to also enjoy the happiness I am surrounded with daily. I cry as I find treasures of Fred and of our marriage. I also smile through those tears. They bring me wonderful memories of good times and of funny times. While some of the memories may be from sad or difficult times, I realize now they were also special because they occurred with Fred. Sometimes we don't know the value of those experiences until we no longer have the opportunity to make more. Again, the yin and the yang and tears of a clown are about the duality of life. The song is about the singer hiding his sadness and tears in public. I interpret the song a little differently; I see it as smiling through the tears of sadness so that some of the tears are also tears of joy at the same time. It isn't an easy thing to do, and I find it takes a tremendous amount of energy to smile through the tears. However, when I do, I feel more balance in my life, and the dark doesn't seem quite so dark and the pain isn't quite as sharp.

I share my story of loss and the Tar Pit with those I seem to connect to throughout my day. It might be a patient going through a similar loss or someone else I meet along the way. I don't share for pity; I share to first connect and then offer hope that despite as bad as it may be, the path through the Tar Pit does eventually get us to the other side. Despite my pain, I find it uplifting and joyful to connect to others at a level I could never have imagined prior to Fred's death. And that is my yin and yang.

God Sightings and Angel Gifts

For as long as I can remember I have been somewhat philosophical and contemplative, and for the record, that can be a blessing and a curse. Sometimes being too contemplative and philosophical can take a person quickly back into the Tar Pit. Thankfully though, my deep thoughts often move me forward through the Tar Pit.

Shortly after Fred died, I received a gift of beautiful wind chimes from a friend. I have always liked the sound of wind chimes and have been fascinated by how many different sounds can be produced by wind chimes of different sizes and shapes. I eagerly hung the wind chimes at the front of my house on a garden arch that Fred had purchased for me and erected. The chimes had a beautiful sound, and I looked forward to hearing them. Oddly, though, where I hung the chimes must have been an area which was protected, and the air seemed to be still even when there was a breeze.

The chimes hung to the right on my patio where I have many flower pots during the spring, summer, and fall. I often would be out on the patio working in my flower beds and flower pots and could feel a breeze but noticed the chimes weren't making a sound. About the time I thought I should move the chimes, there was a day when the air was quite still and yet the chimes made the most beautiful sound. It made me smile. I remember saying out loud, "Hi, honey, I miss you." I can be in the house, and at times, even in still air, I will hear the chimes ring, and I smile at the thought of an angel visit from Fred.

The chimes are not the only God sightings and angel gifts I receive on a regular basis. It may be that I am just more philosophical and contemplative or sensitive to these types of things than usual, but they seem to give me comfort. Several years ago, Fred bought me a large wire moose to display outside at Christmas. (I have a fascination with moose and was thrilled with the gift.) Fred would put the moose outside in early December, and I looked forward to seeing my moose lit up in the December evenings as Christmas approached. Eventually though, the lights didn't work, and we quit putting the moose out as a decoration. The moose was relegated to the loft of our barn.

The first Christmas after Fred died, I needed to find ways to connect with him. The chimes were put away for the winter, and I wanted something else outside to remind me of him. I thought of the moose that Fred bought me and went to the top of the barn and found it. Unfortunately, it was buried beneath multiple cords, cables, etc. As I tried to get the moose loose from the wires and cables, the neck broke. I was horrified!

I started to tear up at the thought of my poor broken moose, a gift from Fred that I had ruined. I thought about fixing my moose with zip ties, many of which Fred often had sitting around the barn or the shop. However, that day, I could not, for the life of me, find a single zip tie. As I looked throughout the many boxes of stuff in the barn and shop, I began to cry and sob. I had broken the moose and now couldn't repair it. I prayed for God to help me, and I talked to Fred to at least show me one lousy zip tie. I looked down, and lo and behold, hanging out of a box at my feet was one zip tie! I could hardly believe what I saw. I quickly repaired my moose and promptly put it outside with a smile through my tears.

We built our house in the early 1990s; Fred died in September 2016. Throughout the years, we had our paper delivered daily, including a Sunday paper. If you do the math, that is quite a few Sunday morning paper deliveries over the course of many years. One Sunday, during the winter of 2016–2017, we had a snowy morning. I was feeling very sad that morning and missing Fred terribly. As I walked out to get the Sunday morning paper, I looked at the end of the driveway, and there were two perfectly shaped hearts in the snow at the end of the driveway. It stopped me in my tracks, and I could not believe what I saw. I had gone out many times throughout many winters to get the paper on a snowy morning, and never were there hearts in the snow. While it was obvious that the hearts were shaped from the paper delivery person's vehicle turning around in my driveway, it was uncanny that it was that particular day, when I was feeling so sad and lonely, that those perfectly shaped hearts showed up. I consider those angel sightings.

I think God sightings are available to recognize all the time; however, we often do not take the time to recognize them. Nicolaus, Lisa and I went to Ireland and England on a trip. It was to be a family trip to also include Fred, Christopher, Michelle, and the grand-daughters. Needless to say, it was not the trip we originally planned, yet it was a wonderful trip, and I feel blessed that we had the opportunity to go. My spot in the car was in the back seat surrounded by luggage. My job was to make sandwiches when needed; it was a fairly low-stress job, and I had plenty of time and opportunity to enjoy the view. A few times, I must admit I was a little melancholy when I longed to have Fred and the rest of the family with us.

One afternoon, I was feeling a little sad and was looking out the window as Lisa drove along and I rode in my assigned place. As I looked up, I saw a beautiful cross of clouds in the sky. I am sure this has happened before, I just never noticed it. While I am much more in tune to these types of God sightings than I used to be, I feel they do actually occur when we need them. God provides for us when He knows we need His special touch.

Several years ago, I started to unclutter my house and began with downsizing my Christmas decorations. I asked my sons if there were items which conjured special memories from their childhood that they would like to have. The few items Christopher wanted I found right away. Nicolaus was given a wooden Nativity set by a neighbor when he was quite young, and he, of course, wanted that. No problem, I put that out every year, and it was easy to find. He also asked for a glass Christmas tree that sat on a musical turntable and changed colors as it turned. I hadn't put that tree out for probably five years, and I looked all over the house for it. I thought that perhaps I had put it in a Goodwill box and gotten rid of it. My heart was heavy because Nicolaus was fond of that tree, and I felt like I let him down. I continued to look for the tree as I put out Christmas decorations to no avail. After Christmas of 2017, I decided I was going to scale back again with my containers of decorations. As I looked around the storage room, my eyes were drawn to a container I was sure did not contain decorations. I hadn't gotten that box off the shelf for years and didn't remember what was in it. I was getting tired and began to walk out of the storage room. As my hand was on the light switch, something made me stop and go back over to the container. It was the oddest feeling, as if someone was leading me to the container. I took a big sigh and began to take the container off a high shelf. I placed the container on the floor, took the lid off, and inside the container in full view was the glass Christmas tree.

I cannot tell you why my eyes were drawn to that container which I had walked by many times the previous years and never felt compelled to look inside. I cannot tell you why I was pulled back to that shelf after I had begun to walk out of the storage room. I can tell you that I do think it was an angel visit, and a sudden peace came over me after I found that tree. I could hardly wait to tell Nicolaus. In fact, I took a picture of it lit up and texted it to him. It now is in its rightful place in its new home with Nicolaus and Lisa.

In the efforts to downsize, I have also begun to drag out and clean up many of the boys' old toys for the granddaughters to play with when they come to visit Grammie. Fisher Price toys, old board games, Little Tikes sets; all are ageless. As I bring them up from the basement or down from the loft of the shop, I think of the many hours of play those toys saw over the years, and I smile. We have a Fisher Price train set that was much beloved, particularly by Christopher. It ran on batteries, and I can still see Christopher loading the train cars up with all sorts of treasures and running them around the track. I dug out the set and cleaned everything up. As I opened the door to place the new batteries in the compartment, I was horrified to find the old batteries still in the train. They were completely corroded in the compartment. I have never seen batteries that badly corroded.

I tried to pull the batteries out, and they fell apart. I tried to dislodge the batteries from the blue-green corroded mess to no avail. I got pliers and screwdrivers to try and dislodge the batteries—nope. I then did what I have become pretty proficient at; I cried. That never is productive and rarely makes me feel better, so I quit crying. If Fred was still alive, I would have placed the train on the table with a note for him to please take care of it, and he "magically" would have fixed it, or at least, that's the story I made up in my head. Obviously, that is not how this was going to play out this time.

As I sat on the floor with newspaper to catch the blue-green powder of the battery corrosion, I found the tiny screws in the train so I could try to open up the train and get the batteries out. I did finally get it loosened enough that I could get my hand inside to pull out the remainder of the batteries. I laughed when I realized that Fred's huge bear-paw-sized hands would have never fit into the battery compartment; I would have had to do it anyway. I would like to say I got the train running again; however, I did not. The corrosion was so bad that the connections were ruined. It reminded me that my "magical thinking" that, if Fred were simply here with me, everything would be perfect again isn't reality based. Things broke and couldn't be fixed when he was alive, and that will continue. Oddly, I found a deep inner strength that day when I realized that sometimes things just break. Sometimes when things break, they can't be fixed, but life can still go on. I think that was an angel gift as well.

Many times, the God sightings and angel gifts aren't things we see; they are feelings we get, similar to a warm hug. Other times, it is a song that comes on the radio or something I am reading that seems to be handpicked for the moment when I am feeling a little sad or just need to feel like Fred is near. There have been times when I am looking for something, similar to the zip tie for the moose or the glass Christmas tree, and I will get a feeling or a thought of where the missing item is located. Lo and behold, when I go to that location, I find the missing item. And sometimes, I just need to be reminded that things break and can't be fixed. While the brokenness makes me sad, it isn't the end of the world and I can be strong despite the brokenness and disappointment.

Fred-and-Karin, Dad-and-Mom—It's All One Word

It's interesting how we are born as individuals and often fight to keep our individuality throughout our childhood, often into adulthood. We strive to be seen as "our own person." Growing up, I soon learned that I was "Mike Wolf's little sister;" rarely did my brother's friends call me Karin. Sometimes I was called "Little Wolfie," but it was clear I was forever united to someone else as part of my identity.

When I started working at Samaritan Hospital, where my mother both graduated from nursing school and worked as a RN and head nurse, I was known for quite some time as "Kay Mosser (Wolf's) daughter." It was through a high school classmate and mutual friend of Fred's that Fred and I met. Many already knew him at Samaritan. He was not only a firefighter on Ashland Fire Department but also a paramedic and regularly brought patients to and from the hospital. After Fred and I got married, I became "Fred Schwan's wife."

I proudly wore the title of Mike Wolf's Little sister, Kay and Fred Wolf's daughter, and Fred Schwan's wife. It was part of my identity. Soon, I would become Nicolaus and Christopher's mom. Of course, I remained my own person, Karin Schwan; however, there was great comfort in being part of my family's identity as well.

I sent, and still send, cards and letters often to friends and family: they include birthday, anniversary, get-well, and sympathy cards. Sometimes I send "thinking of you" cards. I always signed them, "Love, Fred and Karin." Cards to our sons, and then daughters-in-law and grandchildren were from Mom and Dad or Grammie and Papa Schwan. Cards to the nieces and nephews were from Aunt Karin and

Uncle Fred. While there is a space between the words in print, when saying them, it is as if they are one word, one breath, one thought.

After Fred died, the reality that I would have to leave the Fred-and-Karin name and just become Karin again was stark and painful. For years, I would think occasionally about how I would define myself if standing before God. I thought I would say I was a Christian, a daughter, a mother, a sister, a nurse and, yes, a wife. I realized, I was no longer a wife. I was now a widow. I was single. I was no longer "one word." I was "just" me. The reality of that was stark and cold. Something I never felt I would face at fifty-five. How did that happen? I was supposed to be Fred-and-Karin for many more years. That single thought put me deep into the Tar Pit, and it seemed I could not move. At times, I could barely breathe. It wasn't part of my plan, and I didn't like it. I didn't want it.

Funny thing about what we want and what we get. They usually are not the same, and what we get is what we need to learn to deal with if we are to navigate through the Tar Pit. It has been a slow peeling away of Fred-and-Karin. Learning to think in the "me" and not the "we" after being with Fred for over thirty-two years was hard. Learning to talk about "my" house and not "our" house was a difficult reality I did not want to embrace. But as I sat in "my" house by "myself," it didn't matter whether I wanted to embrace the reality that I was alone; that was *the* reality. Fred was not physically there, and he was not coming back. While he would forever be etched in my heart, he was gone and that was what I needed to face.

No matter how much I think I am prepared for times when Fred-and-Karin will present itself, I must admit sometimes I am caught off guard. The mail is one of those triggers for me. I still get mail addressed to Fred, and those things are easily discarded. It has been over a year since Fred's death, and I have converted any active accounts to my name; therefore, things I know will need my attention such as bills come in the mail addressed to me. Mail that comes addressed to Fred and Karin Schwan or Mr. and Mrs. Schwan still makes me pause, and a brief sadness still comes. Address labels are the worst.

For years, "we" gave to multiple not-for-profit causes which has led to calendars, notepads, greeting cards, address labels, etc. The notepads and address labels sometimes come with Fred's name or my name; however, many still come in both our names. When they come, it is a reminder that I am no longer a "Mrs." I still have quite a few notepads with both our names on them, but I continue to purge the Mr. and Mrs. labels. Despite my best efforts to reduce "stuff" around the house, I know I still have hundreds, if not thousands, of sheets of address labels with Mr. and Mrs. Fred Schwan or Fred and Karin Schwan printed on them. It is sad to throw them away, but it is also sad to see them in my basket with my notecards. It seems this is a no-win situation for me.

The random calls for Fred with messages left on my answering machine make me pause and take my breath away. It is even more heartbreaking when I pick up the landline and it is a call for Fred. I explain that he has died and "please take his name off your list" soon follows. I can hear the person on the other end of the phone speechless.

Relationships are fascinating things as they evolve. As a "twenty-something," I embraced becoming Mrs. Fred Schwan, and over the years, we really became "one" as a couple. We pretty much knew what each other was thinking before it was said and what the other would do next. We literally had each other's back in all aspects of life. I liken it to being entwined like a ball of yarn. Now that I am no longer a "Mrs.," I have had to learn how to be single again.

I was twenty-two when Fred and I met and twenty-three when we married. I was fifty-five when I became a widow. We all change as we age, and our experiences and situations change us. While I think part of our basic personality is set early in life, I believe that our relationships with our friends, family, and life partners shape us as well. I truly believe that I am not the same person today as I was when I first started dating and married Fred. As our relationship became more "mature," our personalities somewhat merged. I began to see the world through his eyes, and I somewhat developed his sense of humor. It was difficult, after Fred died, to try and discover where he ended and where I began in our personality traits. I struggled for a while, and then I decided to simply embrace the person that I had become.

Over our many years together, Fred and developed our own language. We, like many couples, knew what the other was thinking before it was said, "got" the inside jokes, and we could tell from a simple look an entire thought stream that was happening in the other person's head. I found I missed that tremendously and was sad at the thought of not having that again with him. The sadness seemed to turn to despair and then anxiety. Who would ever "get" me again? Who would laugh at my jokes and stupid things I did?

Then it dawned on me; I really was still the same person I was when Fred was alive, and when I found something that would have make me chuckle when he was alive, it was still OK to laugh about it. Sometimes I laughed out loud and could imagine what he would have said or done in response to a funny story or joke or something goofy that I did. As I changed my approach, I felt less sad and smiled more and the anxiety lessened. I also began to feel as if I had a part of Fred constantly with me which was comforting. Whether I am Fred-and-Karin, Mom-and-Dad, Grammie-and-Papa-Schwan, Uncle Fred-and-Aunt Karin, or Karin, Mom, Grammie, or Aunt Karin, I am still me, and I realize that I will always carry a big part of Fred in my personality, and honestly…that makes me smile.

The walk through the Tar Pit has gotten easier. Though some days I am amazed at how quickly something can catch me off guard and suck me deep into the pit. I am learning to embrace talking about Fred as both still part of me and yet a separate being. It is difficult to explain and even more difficult for those who have not been through this kind of loss to understand. I appreciate the love and support and attempts to understand though. I have had numerous people tell me, "I just don't know how you do it, I can't imagine if my spouse died," and my response is usually something like this.

"I understand, it was horrible and incredibly painful, but I will tell you that, eventually, you or your partner will have to deal with this. Please do all you can to be prepared."

As I have said before, the reality of life is that we are all born and we all die; it is inevitable. We can either accept that fact and be prepared, or we can bury our head in the sand and pretend we won't have to deal with it. No matter what *we* think, death will eventually come to one of the partners in a relationship. Fred and I were fortunate that we had a few months to get prepared and try to tie up loose ends related to life insurance and finances and our wills. Thankfully, I was fairly well organized; however, I still had more loose ends than I expected.

My best advice to everyone is to please, please have a plan formulated that addresses all the end of life issues you will face prior to needing them. Have a current will, know where your life insurance policies are located in your house, check to see if your accounts are marked as transferable on death, and have current beneficiary information on accounts. Do not pretend that you will not have to deal with the inevitable. You may be the one who dies, but then your partner or spouse or children will be left with the mess if you weren't prepared. Both partners should know how to do the banking, pay bills, and know where the important documents are located. Share what the annual preventative maintenance activities are for your household, whether it is for the heating/air-conditioning, having the septic tank pumped out, checking the household generator, knowing who you use to fix the roof, and the list goes on.

As I continue to learn who "Karin" is again and look back at my time as Fred-and-Karin, I hope to smile more and cry less. I was blessed to have such a strong partner who really was the perfect match for me. He gave me some of the best parts of him during our life together, and I realize it is OK to carry part of him with me always.

Returning to My Roots

As a young woman a.k.a. teenager, I very much enjoyed baking and cooking. I was quite involved in 4-H and took many projects related to cooking, sewing, vegetable and flower gardening, as well as furniture refinishing and natural resources. My spring-summer-fall months were filled with activities such as baking pies and bread, preserving jams and jellies, collecting nuts and leaves from trees, and hiking. I look back fondly on those days and can't believe my mom didn't pull her hair out as I had projects, poster boards, jelly jars, fabric, etc. scattered everywhere.

As odd as it may seem, I think my many activities throughout those formative years prepared me for my Tar Pit path. I learned through these activities to multitask, plan for deadlines, and work under pressure (when I didn't quite plan for the deadlines as well as I thought I did). The Tar Pit and cancer path required some of these same skills as I organized doctors' appointments and radiation treatments, prepared meals ahead of time for Fred when I went to work and someone would come to stay with him, and various other activities that were required to keep everything pulled together as Fred fought the dragon of glioblastoma.

As the summer of 2016 progressed and we were fighting to slay the dragon, I found making strawberry and peach jam, pizza sauce, salsa, and pickles were therapeutic activities. I also made applesauce and grape juice and froze them. The activity kept me focused on something other than Fred's diagnosis and the fact it was obvious he was losing his battle with the dragon. It was as if those activities were part of my therapy.

After Fred died, I lost my desire to do things like cook, bake, shop for groceries, etc. Food wasn't appealing, and performing activities that reminded me of being a wife just made me sad. Over time, though, I found myself drawn back to the kitchen. While I hadn't had time to bake homemade bread for many years prior to starting on the path, I began to feel drawn to bake bread again. There was a sense of comfort in thinking about getting back to my roots of baking and cooking. I found joy in baking, and soon, homemade bread was followed by home-cooked meals. I must admit, eating alone wasn't fun, but I became less focused on being alone and more focused on the joy I found in doing activities which reminded me of happier times.

As I have trudged through the Tar Pit, other activities have become of interest again. The home preserving activities have continued, and I finally have made homemade pizza. My homemade pizza was one of Fred's favorite foods; it ranked right up there with rocky road ice cream. Every time I went to the basement, I would see the jars of pizza sauce sitting in the pantry. It reminded me of my loss, and it became painful to look at the jars let alone think about using the sauce to make pizza. Now I look forward to using my homemade sauce, and I smile as I think of how Fred looked forward to my pizza almost weekly. Sharing pizza with special friends and family is now what I look forward to again.

I haven't returned to refinishing furniture; I just haven't had the time. I find myself looking at projects I will begin to work on once I have the time. At different points in our lives, I think going back to our roots can be comforting—at least it was for me.

Funny thing about roots; we don't usually see roots or think about them. Roots are incredibly important though. They nourish the plant or tree and are the anchor for the plant/tree. Trees that grow in soft soil do not produce deep roots. If you walk through a forest in an area with frequent high winds, you will see that the trees often have grown in the direction that the wind has been blowing them. While they are not growing straight up, they are growing strong, and the roots grow deep to anchor the tree firmly. Our roots are like that: they keep us grounded and standing firm when the storms of life hit. I have found that returning to my roots has given me strength.

Each person needs to find their roots in times of despair and walking the path through the Tar Pit. Part of my roots are deeply grown in my faith. I considered myself a Christian with a strong faith in God and Jesus Christ as my personal Savior. I must be honest though, I don't think my roots had been truly tested by the wind until we received Fred's diagnosis, and we felt as if the wind had been sucked out of us. The impact of that diagnosis was overwhelmingly painful. I could not have imagined anything much worse.

Thankfully, my mother and grandmother planted my roots in faith when I was a young child. And while I grew into adulthood, my faith grew; however, I really don't think it had been greatly tested until Fred's diagnosis. I thought the most difficult thing I had faced to that point was sending our youngest son, Christopher, to Afghanistan. I soon found out that walking the path would require deep roots, and I would need to depend on them to hold me up.

One of my favorite places to visit is in the area of Bishop, California. It is near Yosemite National Park, which I consider heaven on earth. Also very near Bishop is Bristlecone National Forest. I highly recommend a visit to Bristlecone if you really want to get a great visual of roots, wind, and trees. I visited Bishop several months after Fred died and spent some time hiking among the trees in Bristlecone. I was struck at how the trees were twisted and gnarly and yet strong and firmly rooted in the ground. Some of the trees are hundreds of years old and a few are over a thousand years old. These trees have weathered storms, wind, insects, and fire. Ah…the roots, they are the secret to the trees' existence and sustenance.

Being well-grounded and deeply rooted is important. If you have deep roots, be grateful and know that, in times of trouble and grief, it is your roots that can help to sustain you. If you don't feel that you know if you have deep roots, then finding where your roots are located is important, and there is no time like the present to begin to return to them. The winds will blow at some point and struggling to find your roots in a time a turmoil is difficult.

There are opportunities to grow deeper roots throughout our lives. I think sometimes we feel that we are stuck where our roots are planted, and I don't think that's the case. Some of us are firmly planted in good soil and have had an adequate amount of wind to facilitate deep root growth as we face challenges in our lives. I think

I was blessed that way. My grandmother, my mom's mother, died when I was young. I knew very early on in life that she had a tremendous faith. She did not have an easy life, nor did my mom and dad for that matter, and I watched all of them as they faced challenges. Watching others face challenges and keep going helps to grow strong roots. We learn coping patterns from others, particularly those close to us when we are impressionable. Be careful; you never know who is watching and what they are learning from your coping style!

I look at my childhood experiences and realize how fortunate I was that I had those around me who modeled how to face adversity, disappointment, sadness, and deep pain such as that which comes with the death of loved ones. I am keenly aware that not everyone has positive role models during their formative years. The value of sharing stories of adversity and how we overcome the sadness, disappointment, and pain can help ourselves as well as others grow deep roots.

The Tar Pit: One Year Later

The path through the Tar Pit has not been an easy one. I did not start on this path willingly, and I certainly did not expect it to be an easy path to navigate. The Tar Pit is the great equalizer. Rarely do we see ourselves in the same state as others who are going through great loss. We feel sympathy, and at times, we try to empathize, but generally, we are grateful we are not that person, and we usually have no idea how the person feels. To be honest, most of us feel, or certainly hope, "It can't happen to me."

Oh, how the past year has brought me to my knees as I trudged through with fellow Tar Pit dwellers. As I look across the pit, I see those who started out in the pit well before me. Some are far ahead, some I find I am catching up to, and others I see behind me as they dip their toes into the pit, knowing the pain and anguish they are suffering. I can't tell you how often I have used the sight of those ahead to help give me the strength and courage to keep going. I have trudged backward to grab someone behind and pull them forward with me. It really is only a minor setback when realizing that helping someone move forward can be therapeutic for me as well.

At times, I have steadily trudged through the Tar Pit with strong intentions to "just get through it." Again, the pit is a great equalizer. We cannot just will ourselves through the process; we can, however, hold fast to our desire to get through it as we diligently work through the grief. Those are very different things.

While grieving is individual, and each person has their own timeline, there is indeed a timeline. No matter how badly we would just like to be done with the whole process, we have to take the necessary time to get through it or we risk being sucked back into the pit at a depth and distance that may seem insurmountable. In the end, we will be sucked back into the pit at times when we least expect it, but moving forward in the process helps to prepare for being sucked back in, getting our footing, and again beginning to trudge forward.

I never found myself in denial that Fred had died. It was raw, painful, devastating and, honestly, quite awful. Every day when I woke up, it was there in my face as I looked at his pillow. Every night when I went to bed, it was glaringly obvious he was gone and would never return to hug me, to kiss me, or to say, "Hey, kid, how was your day?." I knew I would never get to hold hands with him and run my finger across his wedding band and the calluses from years of working so hard.

I did find, however, that I just wanted the pain to go away, and I wanted to "get through it." Getting through it takes a certain amount of time just like it takes a certain amount of time for a deep wound to heal. We all heal at different rates; however, there is a general standard timeframe for wound healing. I think grief is the same way. We can't take the speed-reading course for grief and get through it in a few short weeks. I tried the speed-reading route; it doesn't work.

The other part of grief that became very obvious quite quickly was that it is overwhelmingly energy sapping. Trudging through thick tar in the Tar Pit is incredibly hard work. Getting out of bed and getting dressed sometimes was like climbing a mountain. Finding energy to think about eating: what to eat, cooking/preparing it, actually chewing and swallowing, and then cleaning up after the meal were monumental tasks some days. Having people ask if I was eating and saying, "You need to take care of yourself," while well-meaning, was not helpful. Once past the initial process of learning about how to eat again is the repeated feeling of loss when eating by yourself. Each meal is a reminder of the loss, so not eating lessens the frequency of the reminders. I knew that was the case in counseling many patients who had lost a spouse, but actually going through it myself was humbling.

So here I am, one year later. If I had the chance to see ahead, through a crystal ball, I think I would have been surprised. I don't think I would have anticipated the emotions, feelings, and how I was coping at this point in time. In one year, I have lost my beloved spouse, watched my family grieve with their loss, watched my beloved mother-in-law die, worked, retired, found new employment, kept the household tasks going, not to mention mowed quite a bit of grass. I have learned to find joy in every day through my continued faith in Christ Jesus and the promise of life everlasting. I have learned to be willing to love again, and find I smile more times than cry. I stop to see a sunrise or a sunset for the joy of the view and wonder how it looks from the other side for Fred. I can do this now without overwhelming sadness and crying and often have a smile on my face, something I could not imagine was possible one year ago.

I still have grief work to do, and my time in the Tar Pit is not done, though I really am ready to get out of the pit. I'd like to be covered in something soft and luxurious that smells good instead of tar. Those days are coming though, and the hope of the future gives me strength to keep moving forward. Fred will always be a part of me, and that makes me smile. I simply would not be the person I am today without him.

Life is a gift; I knew that before, but now it has such a deeper meaning. I am grateful for the days I have been given and feel that, like any gift, it should be treasured and used wisely. And so it goes, this trudging along to get to the edge of the Tar Pit. Looking at those ahead to guide me, those beside me to hold me up, and those behind me to inspire me to carry on ahead as I put one foot in front of the other.

Moving On vs. Pushing Forward

There is a certain amount of comfort of staying in a rut, even if the rut is painful and difficult. A rut can be safe and consistent. I recently was on a flight and sat with an occupational therapist (OT) who works with special needs children; she also works in a psychiatric facility. The other seatmate was a twenty-year-old college student who was heading to a Christian camp for the summer to be a camp counselor. We had a fascinating discussion about personal responsibility, mental health, poverty, and the pain of addiction and grief.

The OT asked the college student, "Do you know what makes people change?"

The college student said, "Because the person wants to do something different?"

The OT shook her head and I said, "It's when the pain and discomfort of staying in the rut becomes greater than the pain of changing."

The OT smiled and said, "Bingo."

The rut and pain of the Tar Pit can be comforting. The pain, while difficult, is consistent; it is a known entity. When we stay in the rut, it means we don't need to put the effort into changing and we don't risk having to face the new and the unknown. I had a friend ask me if I was ready to "give up" the widow role when I made the choice to start dating again. My friend told me the dynamics would change because people would begin to see me as something other than "the poor widow lady." I quickly said "yes" when asked if I was ready for the change. I thought about it more, however, and I realized that though I hated the "widow lady" label, and still do, I have to admit that it was a rut that was safer than learning what the "new me" would look like. The new me is a scary person to know; I haven't really spent many adult years without Fred by my side.

I had a conversation with one of my sons regarding my decision to begin to date again. It intellectually made sense to him. Both of my sons have been so good at realizing that I am still "young" and that being alone the rest of my life may be a very sad way to spend the next potentially thirty to forty years. The heart is a mysterious thing, though, for while it intellectually made sense that I might start dating again, it hurt their hearts deeply at the thought of me being with someone other than their dad. I appreciate my sons' honesty with me and verbalizing that it felt like I was "moving on." While they could never have another dad, I had the opportunity at some point, perhaps, to have a new husband or at least a new "significant other" if I choose to never remarry.

For me, I have never felt that I could really "move on." Staying in the rut, deep in the Tar Pit, is sad, dark and hard; it is also dependable. Feeling sad everyday meant I didn't have to feel happy and then suddenly and unexpectedly be drawn back into feeling sad. Feeling sad all the time seemed less painful. As the time passes and I feel the pain of staying in the rut becoming more overpowering, I realize that I have to push forward through the Tar Pit, and toward making new memories and forming new relationships. The reality though is that, as I work to push forward, I am bringing my sweet, tender memories of Fred with me. I am not dragging him along; I am carrying those memories in my heart.

I call it pushing forward because pushing something is much more difficult than simply moving on through it. Getting out of the rut is difficult and scary. The unknown is not where I have my comfort level; I am a planner. I like to know what is around the bend, and I typically do not like surprises. The effort of pushing forward to what will be the "new normal" of life forever without Fred and learning to develop a new relationship with someone else is incredibly scary.

Some days, weeks, years seem to drag on forever, but the reality is that life is short or ephemeral. We all get a finite number of days on this earth, and my belief is that God expects us to use that time wisely. We are expected to use our time to the glory of God, and that includes making a positive impact on those around us and to share the good news of Jesus Christ. Making public statements about my faith was not something I tended to be comfortable with until Fred's diagnosis. I thought simply believing in God and Jesus and "trying to do the best I could" in living a life that God expected was enough. That thinking and acting was a comfortable rut. It was safe and consistent and not very controversial. Fred's diagnosis changed everything though. He and I felt that our faith that God would sustain us through whatever was to come was something we needed to share openly. I watched him bravely face certain death with so much class and dignity. We received such words of encouragement from others as we publicly shared our walk of faith. Both Fred and I came out of our rut in our walk with God and pushed forward into the unknown territory of blind faith that God would sustain us and provide.

Pushing forward is still so hard for me, and at times, I am exhausted in trying to keep forward progression. At times, I want to run back deep into the Tar Pit so the darkness can swallow me up and I can once again get comfortable in the rut of pain and grief. I realize, though, that God expects better of me, and I think Fred does too. He was never one for feeling sorry for himself, and I believe he wouldn't expect me to sit around feeling sorry for myself either. I can hear him saying, "Kid, you need to push forward through this. Time is short, and you always want to accomplish so much. Wasting time in a rut isn't good for you."

I wish getting out of the rut was easier. I enjoy working hard, but I like to be able to visually see the fruits of my labor. When I work hard to get my garden in every year, I am rewarded by vegetables that sustain me. When I work hard cleaning the barn or the garage or…gulp…the basement, I am rewarded by seeing a neater, cleaner space. I can't physically see the transit through the Tar Pit and the forward progression out of the rut. I am a visual person, so seeing results is important to me. Learning that I can't always see the results but have to go by faith and feel is new and uncomfortable, but I am learning that the pain of staying in the rut is greater than taking the leap of faith in pushing forward.

A part of me wants so badly to stay in the current and past chapters of my life. I was comfortable in those chapters; I had a husband who loved me despite all my flaws and neurotic tendencies. I had predictable unpredictability with a man who worked hard and played hard and was always up for an adventure with me. I had a job at a hospital where I worked for thirty-five years, and while I admit I didn't always love my job, I always liked the people I was blessed to work with for many years. The current chapter in the Tar Pit is one of predictable sadness, and while I truly hate the Tar Pit, it is a necessity to trudge through to come out into a new chapter in my life. The hard work of grief is just that—hard work.

New chapters are hard to start. As I have worked on this book, I struggle to start each one: What title will I use that will be catchy but not sound stupid? What do I write that will be meaningful but not reveal so deeply into my soul that it seems forced or insincere? How long do I make my chapters, and when will I have put enough thoughts and feelings into words that people will find it worthwhile to read this book? It may be that as I pour out my thoughts and feelings, this will stay just a folder in my computer, and it never will come to fruition as a published book.

The reality of all of this is that our book of life does continue to move forward as it is written. We can either complete the chapters as they go by and relish what was in them, looking forward to the next chapter ahead, or we can bemoan that we have finished a chapter and that we don't want to complete the book or the story. We are given the task to live life intentionally or it will pass quickly and end with little meaning. The certainty of life is that it begins and ends, and what we do with the time we have between those two certain events is the stuff that leaves the chapters of our book of life for others to read. We can simply move through the days of our lives in a rut or we can push forward through the days despite pain, knowing that we are writing chapters which may inspire and guide others. I think living intentionally to write meaningful chapters is what God expects of us, and those who have passed through the thin veil to eternity are cheering us on to do.

I look forward to my daily devotionals. I feel out of sorts all day when I miss my morning routine of devotionals, praying, and asking God to give me guidance and discernment. I have several verses and inspirational messages I read each day during this time as well. One message is, "God sends us His vertical support through horizontal help of others." I find this comforting that those who offer me comfort and guidance are heaven-sent. I also find it inspiring that I am to do the same for others.

I have learned that, despite my best efforts and wishes, I cannot get through this life on my own. For years, I felt I was independent and really did not need to depend on others. I realize now it was a façade. It is humbling to learn that no matter how hard I try to control my environment, emotions and, yes, even others, I truly am frail and powerless without the love and support, first from God, and then from others. I can look at this as weakness, or I can feel empowered by the fact that none of us can do this on our own.

When I look around at this broken world, it seems to me that much of the problem with substance abuse and suicide is related to understanding relationships with each other, with God, and with ourselves. We are given a false view in society that everything should be easy and we should be able to have whatever we want in life and that life should be happy and pain free. The reality is this: life is hard and painful at times. As the saying goes, "No man is an island," even though some of us like to think we can be independent and do not need to depend on others.

The corollary of learning to depend on others is also that we need to be dependable for others. How we interact with those around us makes an impact. It is up to us to decide whether we will choose to give those around us a positive experience or not. Of course, it is up to those who interact with us to decide how they will react to the experience. We have all had experiences where it ends with the thought, "Well, that didn't go as planned."

I know that as I continue to push forward, I will continue to need the love and support of others. My nature is to push forward with my head down and just move forward. I am learning every day that, though this has been my usual mode of operation, it isn't what will sustain me. I cannot do this alone, and I realize that despite all the heartache and pain of learning to live without Fred, it is a gift to learn to depend on others and to hold tightly to God's words daily.

Sunrises, Sunsets, the Thin Veil, and a Big Fish

Many of us enjoy watching a great sunrise or a beautiful sunset. Often people spend time watching cloud formations throughout the day. Some enjoy watching the sky as a storm is looming or when lying in the grass looking up at the sky as a way to pass the time and play games of "what do I see." Fred loved a great sunrise or sunset, and we often talked about them at the end of our day when we finally had a chance to connect. When Fred worked summers as a school custodian, he went in early to beat the heat of the day since the school wasn't air-conditioned. He still had the mowing business to keep going in the afternoon and evening, and getting to the school early meant he could finish his day there and mow. The drive to the school was heading east, and he really enjoyed seeing the early beams of light come over the hillsides on his way to the school. Sometimes he would text me to look at the sunrise as soon as I was up and getting ready for work. I felt a special connection with him through our discussions about the sunrises and sunsets; it was common ground when we often spent so much time apart.

When Christopher was in Afghanistan, I struggled with my anxiety about his safety. I missed that kid so much. I coped in several unique ways including canning quite a bit of pickles, jams and jellies, salsa, and pizza sauce. For some reason, I found home preserving and painting most of the rooms in the house therapeutic. Another way I found solace in my anxiety-ridden times was to stop every morning when I walked Sasha, Christopher's dog, and look at the sunrise. With the time difference between Ohio and Afghanistan, I envisioned that as I enjoyed the sunrise, he was nearing sunset and one more day closer to coming home. At sunset, I did the same and used it as a way to pause to pray for his safe return. Each morning and night brought a reduction in my anxiety level. It made me feel closer to him.

Fred and I had a wonderful trip of a lifetime to Australia and Fiji in April 2016, just prior to his diagnosis. I am simply amazed he did as well as he did, particularly considering the size of the brain tumor. For him to have snorkeled, used a new camcorder, hiked to the top of the Sydney Harbor Bridge and back down again, and kept the pace as we traveled for almost two weeks still shocks me. By all accounts we should not have been able to go on the trip due to his health. We didn't get our miracle cure; however, I really feel that the trip happened at all was a miracle. Then to think back on the absolutely stunning sunset view we enjoyed on the beach, in Fiji, as we celebrated Fred's birthday, I am simply awestruck. The picture I took of him standing with his arms out and the setting sun behind him is a favorite; it also seems it was a portent of things to come.

Since Fred's death, I find myself drawn even more so to watching for a great sunrise or sunset as well as looking at the night sky for stars and shooting stars and enjoying the many phases of the moon. I have spent a great deal of time standing out in the yard, looking up and talking to God and Fred. I ask God to give me peace and strength to continue my path through the Tar Pit. I tell Fred about my day and tell him I hope he is proud of me for trying to keep trudging along. I share funny stories of the stupid things I do or what I was able to get accomplished around the yard or in the house. I tell him every day how much I love him still and how much I miss him. I feel close to him when I am looking at the sky. I wonder if he is looking down, and if so, I wonder what his view looks like from heaven above.

One might wonder how I could have a fish in the title of this essay when it has been about the night sky and the sun. I am happy to explain. The summer of 2016 was a really, really difficult one for all of us, particularly Nicolaus and Christopher. They were scrambling to spend time with their dad, offer me emotional support, and work at their full-time jobs. Nicolaus was trying to run the lawn business, and Lisa helped him when she could. Lisa also helped me by stopping to check on Fred before his radiation "team buddy" would pick him up, or she would bring him to me at work so we could head to the treatment from there. Christopher was working and trying make it back to our house as often as possible and took his dad for treatments as well, and had a very pregnant wife, Michelle, and preschooler at home too. Despite all the chaos, the boys found a way to take their dad fishing. For some reason, Fred was obsessed about fishing; apparently, the brain tumor triggered something that made him want to fish. The boys scrambled to pull off a fishing trip with a man who was confused and had to be reminded what to do with the pole. Nicolaus, Fred, and Steve Cellar, who graciously offered his boat for the trip, fished from the boat, and Christopher fished from his kayak. It was a challenge to keep Fred focused, but he did get to fish, and although it was bittersweet for all involved, they had a good time. Fred told the boys that the next time they went fishing at Charles Mill, they needed to go to the exact spot they were that day and "a big fish would be waiting." Ramblings of a man with a large brain tumor...

Fast forward to August 2018, Nicolaus and Christopher decided to go fishing in the boat that Nicolaus and I had purchased for Fred years ago but that he rarely used due to working so hard. The motor was old and undependable and hadn't started since 2016. The boys were going to use kayaks to fish from as a backup in the event the motor wouldn't start. Nicolaus gave the motor some pre-trip TLC but was doubtful that he would be able to get it started. He also needed to find the boat registration which had gone AWOL since 2016 as well. The closer it got to the fishing trip, the more it seemed it would be a disappointment. My heart ached, for I wanted this to be a fun brother-bonding time and not a sad reminder that they didn't have their dad with them.

The day of the trip arrived, and Nicolaus was still looking for the registration to no avail. He decided to check the tackle box one more time, even though he had previously checked multiple times. Lo and behold, there was the missing document! The boys headed out with the boat and kayaks, certain that the motor wouldn't start but hoping, somehow, it would. Once the boat was in the water, it took two pulls and the motor started. After two years of sitting idle, it started on just two pulls. Off the boys went on their fishing trip. The day was very hot, not a good one for fishing. Christopher was using his dad's pole and caught a large fish, so large that it broke the line but, thankfully, not the pole. They said they watched the bobber for about an hour as that large fish swam around dragging the line. As the day went on, they caught a few fish but nothing spectacular. Before deciding to call it a day, the boys decided they would hunt for the location where they fished with their dad. After going to the other side of the lake, they found the location and the channel where Fred told them a big fish would be waiting. You guessed it! Nicolaus caught a rather large catfish and reeled it in. He said it was outstanding eating that night.

Sometimes we cannot explain how and why things happen, both good and bad. I think we aren't supposed to always understand, we simply have to have faith. At times, I truly can feel Fred's presence just beyond my reach, but it is still there. Sometimes I find something, such as the zip-tie for the Christmas Moose repair job, when I think I just can't look anymore. Sometimes a sunset, sunrise, stars, and the moon make us feel close to one who is so far away. And sometimes, a big fish is waiting for us in the exact location we were told it would be by a man who is missed so very much. I call these "thin veil" moments.

In some writings about heaven, it explains that when we die, we move through the thin veil where others who have gone before us welcome us to heaven. We are told it is joyous occasion that is beyond comprehension. It seems to me if it is just a thin veil away, it is also only thin veil separating us, and at times, we can feel our loved one's presence through it. So the sun, moon, stars, a beautiful sunrise, a gorgeous sunset and, yes, a big fish give me comfort as I long to hear Fred's voice or hold his hand. I may not get to touch him, but I truly do feel his presence at times through the thin veil.

Finding Me Again and My True North

I think when we are with someone for years, we begin to become tangled into their inner being. That's what makes a relationship so wonderful—at least it was that way for Fred and me. We knew how the other would react, what the other would do, and how to complete each other's sentences. We had an understanding that didn't need words. We could look at each other across the room and know what the other was thinking or feeling. Many people call that having a soulmate. There was great comfort for me having someone who loved me despite all my oddities, foibles, insecurities, and quirkiness. Sometimes I wasn't sure if Fred loved me despite all my flaws or because of them, but one thing was certain; he loved me unconditionally. And I loved him unconditionally.

When you lose a partner that is so much a part of you, you lose a part of you as well. It takes some time to figure out again who you are and where you are headed. Years ago, I bought a book called *True North*. Oddly, I remember reading the book, but I can't remember exactly what I read. I do know it wasn't one of those books about finding your moral compass, it was more about finding our way through the rough times in our lives and looking to our "true north."

Quite a while back, a friend and I decided we wanted do something different, and we signed up in the fall for a "becoming an outdoors woman" weekend put on by the Ohio Division of Wildlife. It took place on a weekend from Friday afternoon to Sunday at noon. We stayed in a dorm setting and had options for multiple sessions both outdoors and in the lodge. Options were quite varied, including campfire cooking, basic canoeing, archery, gun safety, animal tracking, fishing, and orienteering. This was well before the geocaching craze.

I took an archery session, as well as several others, but the one that sticks with me is the orienteering course where we learned to use a compass. I wanted to take up archery after this, so Fred and I checked out various bows; we didn't know if I should use a "regular one" or if using a crossbow would work better for me. In the end, I didn't pursue it further, which is a shame, and who knows, maybe that will be my next hobby. I think I am a collector of hobbies and thus may never have time to devote to become an archer.

Fred bought me a nice compass that year at Christmas. I used it for a while but never got very good at reading a topographical map. He tried so hard to teach me. I don't know why, but it was difficult for me to read the map, use my compass, and figure out where I was and where I was going. I wish I could find that compass now.

Despite the fact that I never took up archery, I never became competent in compass orienteering and am still learning about kayaking and target shooting, I did walk away from all my attempts to "become an outdoors woman" with the sense that, despite failures and a less than a stellar performance, keeping my eyes focused on my true north is important. For years, I thought my true north involved being a good wife and mother. I thought I had gotten at least reasonably competent in those two roles; I certainly wasn't the best, but I had a strong marriage, and our sons were growing into really fine young men.

Over the years, I have had many different hobbies. Some of them I became fairly capable at doing such as gardening, sewing, hiking, and furniture refinishing. I have had other hobbies I have tried but never became what I would call competent at doing such as knitting, crocheting, and painting. I came to terms with the fact that I am not good at many things, but there are a few things I was capable of doing in a reasonably competent manner.

In my professional life, I have had the opportunity to be involved in multiple areas of nursing. Fred was always very proud of the many things I was involved in throughout my nursing career, but what he was most proud of was my role as diabetes educator. He would freely share with strangers as well as acquaintances and friends that I was a diabetes educator if he found out they had diabetes. Anyone who knew Fred knew he loved to eat and struggled with his weight most of his adult life. He would tell people, "Don't look at me and judge Karin's ability to teach based on my weight. She is good. I just choose not to listen." (He was a funny man with a really great sense of who he was and who he wasn't. I loved that about him.)

I don't know for certain, but I think Fred had a pretty good sense of his true north and where his compass was leading him. He was so content being a great husband and father as well as a terrific son, brother, and uncle. He loved being a firefighter, and I truly believe that was his destiny. He loved his God, Jesus, and he knew where he was headed when he died.

I jokingly have said, "Ye who dies first wins." (I explore this in depth in another essay.) The spouse who dies first doesn't have to try and sort out the earthly stuff accumulated over the years together, the financial issues, or the pain of being the one left. Once we are with God, we have "the wisdom of the Lord;" we don't have to figure out who we are and where we are headed. God is the ultimate true north, and our faith is our compass.

Losing the role as wife has been devastating. I wore that title so proudly, and while I believed someday I would not have Fred on earth me with anymore, I never imagined he would die at age sixty-three. I am pretty good at planning, and this was not part of my plan. That's the thing about plans; it's always good to have a plan B, and I did not have one. That is also the thing about plans; we can always make new ones.

I am in the process of finding "me" again since the definition of me changed quite dramatically on September 22, 2016. I continue as a mother, a sister, a daughter, and aunt and, now, a grandmother. I will always be a nurse whether I am actively practicing or not, and I suspect I will be a diabetes educator for many more years to come. I can see Fred smiling as he tells people how proud he was of me in that role.

My true north will always be God and Jesus Christ as my Savior. While I can't use an actual compass to figure out where my true north lies, I think the Bible is *the* compass we all need to use. Even so, I struggle daily as a sinner in figuring out how to get my journey mapped out. I have no doubt that I will go to heaven when I die, not because of anything I have done but because Christ died for me. My job is to accept that and believe that Christ is the narrow gate through which we must pass in order to be in heaven with Him.

If I ever find the compass Fred gave me, I think I will try to take orienteering again as a hobby. I am not sure I will ever feel capable and competent enough to go off on my own with a compass and a topo map, but if I can find my way around locally, I will call it a success. I am still trying to find the new me, and I suspect that will take quite a bit of time as I focus on my true north. I am not sure we ever really know we have arrived at our true north until the end of our lives. I can only imagine the treasures waiting for us in heaven when we arrive; it's a heavenly form of geocaching, I suppose.

Hands Dripping with Honey

As some are aware, cancer begins as one single cell goes awry, at least most of the time. We constantly have cells that become abnormal, but we have "killer cells" in the body that recognize those "bad guys" and kill them—the scientific word for this is apoptosis. It's funny, I do not remember this ever coming up in nursing school, but it was discussed quite a bit by my professor in grad school in the Pathophysiology class. (Pathophysiology was always one of my favorite subjects.) A rogue cancer cell rarely is the problem; however, multiple cells can begin to overwhelm the body's defenses, and eventually, changes occur to the point that cancer is diagnosed.

Why is the evolution of cancer included in this essay? Well, it's all about timing. When Fred had his first brain biopsy to confirm that it was glioblastoma multiforme, I asked his surgeon how long he thought Fred had the tumor. He stated it was a fast-growing type of cancer, and he doubted that he had it more than five to six months prior to his diagnosis in early May 2016. Simple math in my head took me back to November/December of 2015 when the rogue cells began and soon would overtake his body's ability to kill them. I looked at the family picture we had taken at Christmas 2015 and wondered if the cells were present at that time, hiding and waiting to overtake his ability to fight them.

I will back up a few years to 2013. Christopher, our youngest son, deployed to Afghanistan in the spring. I was busy with work, shipping care packages to Afghanistan, gardening, and doing anything to keep my mind off our son so far away in harm's way. An opportunity came up through Trinity Lutheran Church in Ashland, where we were members, and a Lutheran Church in Ethiopia to partner together to serve the poorest of the poor in remote villages in

Ethiopia. Fred and I went to the informational meeting, and the group discussed possibilities, including a medical mission team trip. We had done a mission trip to Kenya together and a youth mission trip to North Carolina with Christopher, but we had not done a medical mission trip. We left the meeting intrigued but decided we had too much on our plates to do it.

God has His plan, and if we listen to the still small voice He speaks inside of us, we find His plan may be different from ours. In the end, I decided that I would assist in pulling a team together and would take a leap of faith and go to Ethiopia. Fred would hold the fort down at home, particularly since the trip was planned for the end of January, which is prime snowplowing season, and he had his business to run. Even though he had the snowplowing business to worry about, he willingly helped with transportation needs. He would be the one to drive us and all of our stuff to the airport in the wee hours of the morning. Fred would also pick us up, exhausted, when we came home.

The first year I went was particularly emotional. A group of eleven of us traveled from the United States to Ethiopia. Two had been in the Peace Corp and served in Ethiopia, and one participant was born there but had been living in the United States for years. The remaining eight of the group had not been to the country previously. None of us had done a medical mission trip like this, and we truly were walking on faith. Just before we left, our beloved Dad Rogers became quite ill and was hospitalized. As I told him goodbye the night before I flew to Ethiopia, I was not sure that he would be alive when I got back. On top of that, Christopher was to come home about the time I was to return, and I was heartbroken at the fact I might not be back in time to make his welcome home ceremony. God's plan is God's plan, so off we went as a team, including our daughter-in-law Lisa, Nicolaus's wife.

I think I could write a whole book on the three medical mission trips we took in 2014, 2015, and 2016. Each time, all of us grew personally, professionally, and spiritually. I believe that God planted His seed of hope and strength for me well before the rogue cancer cells began to multiply in Fred's brain. He was teaching me to be stronger and push through difficult times, even when I thought I couldn't do it.

When we returned to the United States in 2014, and could use our cell phones, it was such a relief to find out that Dad Rogers had rallied and was in a local rehabilitation facility. I also got the news that Christopher made it back safely to the United States but was still in Mississippi. I had not missed his coming home ceremony, and I would get to see Dad Rogers soon! Christopher arrived back in Ohio on February 14, and he too got to see his grandfather before he died in late March. Mom and Dad Rogers were able to celebrate their twenty-fifth wedding anniversary surrounded by family before he went to be with his heavenly family. God's timing is truly amazing.

The 2015 medical mission trip was totally different from the previous one and seemed more stressful; the travel was difficult, and the living conditions were harsher than the previous year. Of course, we still had better conditions than most of the people we were treating, so it's hard to really complain. I am not sure if that contributed to my heavy heart as I prepared for the 2016 trip or if something inside me knew that something bad was coming.

The trip actually went well. By the third year, the team had a pretty good system, and we were blessed to be working with an amazing group of local people in Ethiopia. Each day on our trip to the location where we would set up our clinic, several of the Ethiopian ladies would read scripture and pray for us. If you were among the lucky ones who got to ride in their van, you couldn't help but feel spiritually full by the time of arrival at the clinic site. The drive time varied depending on the location, but generally it was an hour of concentrated time worshipping God. The ladies did not speak English, so they would read and pray, and someone would translate so we could understand.

Near the end of our week together, the ladies began to tell us of their visions for each of us. They were emotional times of scripture reading, prayer, and translating the visions they had for each individual. Oddly, I do not remember the exact scriptures read for me, but I do remember that the ladies spoke repeatedly about my "hands dripping with honey," and they cried loudly as they read the scripture. I cried too, but I cried for joy as I interpreted it that my hands were used for tending to the sick all week, and that was the metaphor for the vision. I was exhausted and homesick, and this made me feel that, at least, I had hopefully made a difference in the lives of those I touched. I also had taken jars of honey as gifts for the local staff we worked with, so of course, I thought that was the reason for the vision of my hands with honey as well. Done...or so I thought. When we arrived back in Columbus, Fred was there to pick us up and bring us home. And as usual, he had spent the whole time we were gone plowing and salting, and he was tired. He seemed more tired than usual though, and we didn't have much time to regroup because we had to get ready for our trip of a lifetime to Australia and Fiji in April. We had our tax return information to get collected as well as the prep required for international travel. There would be no down time.

Fred never particularly embraced working on the taxes. I must admit that was a bone of contention almost every year. I am a "get it done early" kind of girl, and he was a "get it done just in time" kind of guy. However, 2016 was different; he seemed so unfocused and scattered that we both chalked it up to being tired and excited about the trip. He did get his business financials pulled together though, and we were able to get the information to our tax preparer in time to have everything done before we left for Australia early in April.

Traveling halfway around the world is exhausting at best. In addition, our flights were certainly not optimal, so we arrived extremely worn out in Cairns, Australia. We both recovered quickly and had a wonderful time. Right before we left on the trip, Fred bought a small camcorder. He was never a "techie" guy, so I really thought he wouldn't be able to figure out how to use it, but he surprised me and took great video. I treasure it since he narrated the scenes, and I love to hear his voice.

The trip ended with several days in Fiji. While both of us were excited about going to Fiji, we really always wanted to see New Zealand and Australia. This trip included Fiji instead, and we were happy to be able to go on the trip. We were there over his sixty-third birthday, which ended up being his last one on earth. I tried to plan a special sunset boat ride for us, but it wasn't available, so instead, I booked a gourmet dinner for two on the beach at sunset on his birthday, April 17. It was the most beautiful sunset we had ever seen, and even the locals remarked that they had never seen one so beautiful. Again, God has impeccable timing.

By the end of our time on Fiji, Fred was so incredibly tired, but we chalked it up to the heat and humidity as well as his high blood pressure that we thought was out of control due to the heat and the trip itself. As we headed home, he admitted he felt a little confused at the airport in LA, but we had been up for almost twenty-four hours, and I was a little disoriented as well. Things would quickly deteriorate once we got home, and less than three weeks later, he was in the James Cancer Center at OSU Medical Center having a brain biopsy for cancer.

I still have difficulty wrapping my head around 2016. It seemed to have flown by in a blink of an eye, and yet time seemed to have stood still as well. I look back now at all the subtle signs and wonder if I had paid more attention or hadn't been trying to do too many things if I would have realized the symptoms sooner. Perhaps if we intervened sooner, the rogue cancer cells could have been stopped; that's the thing about hindsight giving us 20/20 vision. While I know, intellectually, I had no control over the outcome, I can't help but feel a little guilty that I couldn't do more to save Fred.

You may be asking about the "hands dripping with honey" vision and how it all ties in. It wasn't until I began posting Fred's cancer path on Facebook that I thought about the vision again. I was so busy after returning from Ethiopia in early February that I could only think of everything that needed to get done to catch up from being gone and get ready for the next adventure. As I began to get feedback from people telling me how my posts affected them and Fred's faith and strength gave them strength as well, I realized that the "honey" was the story my hands were typing to share. I can't tell you exactly when that enlightened moment came, but I can say I cried long and hard when I realized it. I then understood why the ladies were so emotional and why the long and tight hug I received from them as we said goodbye was different than the hugs from them the two previous years.

As I told people I was going to write a book someday about "the path" and "the tar pit," I received a great deal of encouragement. As I write, I really don't know if the book will ever get published, but it is cathartic and healing for me to share the story. I hope that if others do read this someday that it helps them as they walk their own path through the tar pit.

Learning to Breathe Again

As I have written my individual essays I have thought, "*Well, this will be the last one*, and yet I continue to have thoughts about Tar Pit dwelling and my path through it swirling in my head. I do my best thinking when I am walking. Many of the topics have come as I have been walking and thinking and watching the sunset or sunrise or the clouds. This topic is no different.

Most of us at one time or another have probably had "the wind knocked out of us." It is a feeling like we will not be able to catch our breath again, and even though we know we aren't going to die, it certainly feels that way for a while. It is both painful and scary, but it does pass, and we catch our breath and soon go on our way.

Breathing is an interesting activity. It is something we do day in and day out, and we usually don't think about it unless we have some type of respiratory problem or we feel out of breath due to running or other heavy exertion or…we get the wind knocked out of us. Thankfully, we don't have to control our diaphragm for each breath or we would get nothing else done let alone we would never be able to sleep.

When I got the call with the results of Fred's MRI of his brain showing the tumor, I felt like I had been kicked in the stomach and that the wind had been knocked out of me. I really could not catch my breath. It was as if I simply would not be able to breathe again. I remember sitting down and hanging up the phone and realizing that I had to get a plan together quickly. I took a deep breath and off I went to the hospital to get copies of his MRI so I could take him and the MRI down to the James Cancer Center at OSU.

For me, breathing relates very closely to how I see my relationship with Fred and my path through the Tar Pit. Fred and I met when I was twenty-two, and we married when I was twenty-three. I spent most of my formative adult years with him. I became so used to having him in my life it was just like breathing. I treasured each breath, but I didn't think about breathing constantly. My time with Fred was much the same way; I treasured my relationship with him but didn't think of it constantly. My relationship with Fred was like breathing, in and out, so natural, so comfortable. Ah, but just like breathing, when you have a bad cold or run hard, when there is a rough spot in a relationship, you think more about it and it gets difficult. You think about breathing, you feel the pain sometimes through the difficulty, and then you treasure the easy, quiet breaths when the difficulty subsides. In and out, easy and peaceful…that's how breathing usually goes for us most of our days. We take our life-sustaining breaths for granted most of the time; it's human nature to do so. It also is what we tend to do with our really good relationships.

Then the "sucker punch" happens. We are caught off guard when the wind is knocked out of us. We feel the pain, the terror of not being able to catch our breath. We panic and we also think about breathing on a new level. It becomes very conscious and purposeful to take the next breath. We struggle to get the next breath so we can continue on. I struggled so hard the day of the diagnosis to catch my breath, May 9, 2016. I truly remember it like it was yesterday.

As I have continued through my Tar Pit dwelling and walking the path to get at least to the edge of it, I have had days when I simply felt I could not breathe anymore. It was as if each moment I was being "sucker punched," and the wind was being continually knocked out of me. The struggle to breathe both physically and metaphorically was great. There are days, though, when I breathe and do not think about it; it is easy and quiet and there is no struggle.

If I could tell Fred one thing, it wouldn't be that I love him. I believe he really did know how much I always loved him, and still do, and I did get to tell him that many times before he died. I would like to tell him, though, that I took him for granted just like I take breathing for granted most days. I was so comfortable in my relationship with him, just like the comfort of breathing most of the time. I would tell him I took for granted just how special of a relationship that we had. It seemed so common to me, just like breathing, but it was to be treasured just like the gift of breath.

As the days go by, I don't feel like I have had the wind knocked out of me quite as often, and when I do, I recover more quickly. I must admit that when it happens, it quickly pulls me back out deeply into the Tar Pit. It then takes a while to catch my breath and begin the forward progress again. It is mentally and physically exhausting to remember to "just breathe" as the next wave hits in the Tar Pit. I think for those who are in their own Tar Pits, it is important to realize the amount of energy expended day to day facing and dealing with grief and to be kind and understanding to ourselves. For those walking along in support through the Tar Pit, please understand how exhausting the path through the Tar Pit is; please be patient. For those waiting on the edge of the Tar Pit, be gentle as we get near the edge; we can barely catch our breath as we see the shore.

As I take my walks, I find comfort most of the time in thinking of nature, of God's gifts, of how blessed I have been despite my loss. Most days, my walks involve me contemplating what has happened and looking forward to the future, and I don't think about breathing. I must admit that occasionally my walks lead to a "sucker punch," and I must remind myself to just breathe as I continue to work through this thing called grief and walk the path through the Tar Pit.

The Tire
Part 1

I knew I was fortunate to have Fred as my mate, and I knew I was spoiled by him. I often told people how lucky I was that he was my husband, and I truly believed it, but I must admit I didn't really know how spoiled I was until after Fred was diagnosed. When I had to take over his chores and all the little things he did, I soon was overwhelmed.

My first "adventure" into being "the man of the house" as well as continuing to be "the woman of the house" was mowing the lawn the summer of 2016. Even though Fred had a lawn-mowing business and we had several lawn mowers, I did not mow our lawn at home. Fred's belief was that I worked full-time, took care of quite a few things around the house, and I "shouldn't have to mow the lawn too." I think a little of the reason for him not wanting me to mow is that he knew I would not mow to his standards. I suppose that saved us both some stress, and that was a great concept until he couldn't mow the lawn and I didn't know how to use the tractors/ mowers. I did have several wonderful friends come and mow the lawn, which was particularly helpful when the grass was extremely long. The kids helped when they could, but they were overwhelmed as well. Eventually, Nicolaus brought me a cordless push mower, and I used it for most of the rest of the mowing season. Oh my word!!! I live in the country, and hand mowing several acres of yard was quite a workout. I also learned to use my cordless trimmer.

Subsequent "adventures" would test my moxie more than my physical endurance like the hand mower did, and I knew I had more tests to come. I had been independent in taking my car for oil changes and routine maintenance. I had had not learned to change a tire; however, I do have AAA, so at least I have a backup plan. Shortly after Fred died, I was driving to the grocery store when I heard a strange noise coming from the left front tire. When I parked the car, I found a large screw deeply embedded into the tire, but the tire wasn't flat, at least yet. I panicked and immediately started crying, and so I called Nicolaus, who was on duty and unavailable to come and help me. He suggested that I call a local garage and ask if I could drive my car to the garage to have the tire checked out. I called Travis at the garage, who I hoped would be able to help me. The poor man, as soon as I heard his voice, I started sobbing, and he was so sweet and understanding. He told me to head to the garage but, if anything went wrong, to pull over and call him back and he would send a tow truck immediately. I drove slowly with the *thump-thump* sound of the screw in the tire barely drowning out my sobbing and arrived safely. Travis assessed the damage to the tire, and interestingly, he could not find the screw, and the tire was not damaged. It was if an angel had interceded for me. I had a sense of calm come across me as I drove home; I survived my crisis.

Next on the agenda was dealing with the whole house generator. For months prior to Fred's diagnosis, I had been telling him that the generator wasn't performing the weekly auto checks. He kept telling me it was working fine. We left on vacation, and I forgot about the generator. Shortly after our return, Fred's symptoms rapidly let us know something was terribly wrong, and from that point until after his death, I didn't think about the generator. Shortly after his death, though, it dawned on me that I hadn't heard the generator for quite some time, and when I checked on it, the "dreaded red light" was lit, indicating that there indeed was a problem with the generator. And so began the efforts to get the generator fixed. I also needed to figure out who to call to get the propane tank filled for the generator. All of this normally would have been seamlessly handled by Fred. The man who showed up to fix my generator and the man who fills my propane tank were sweet, patient, and understanding. More than once, I broke out into tears as they instructed me on what to do. I kept thinking that Fred should still be here with me and I didn't want to deal with all of this. They could see I was struggling with trying to do everything I needed to do, and I was blessed to have understanding people around me who wanted to help. Maybe they just wanted me to stop crying, but I will give them the benefit of the doubt.

Anyone who owns, rents, or lives in a house, which is the majority of us, knows that ongoing maintenance of our homes is inevitable. My house is no different, the difference is that usually I could ask Fred, ask Fred again, leave a list, and then ask again, and eventually get whatever needed done fixed. It's interesting when the list you make is solely for yourself and you realize that you are the one who will deal with the issue(s). The *click-click* of the garage door opener with no movement of the garage door was my next crisis. Fred would have handled it. I had no idea who he used for previous installation and maintenance of the garage door openers. I looked through the yellow pages of the phone book—yes, that still exists—but nothing struck a familiar chord. As I opened the famous "junk drawer" looking for something else, I found a business card for Magic Door. I didn't remember seeing the card in the drawer before, but there it was, almost jumping out of the drawer at me. I called Magic Door and indeed, "we" were their customer, and they came out to fix my garage door opener. I am not amazed that Magic Door fixed my garage door opener—after all, that is their business. I am amazed though at how the business card was there in the drawer at the very moment I needed it.

I continue to learn to improvise, make contacts about ongoing household maintenance, and learn how to deal with new things that haven't come up previously. Sometimes I find notes in the desk that Fred left helping me to know who to call or what to do. Sometimes I struggle with what to do and who to contact. I have found that I am more capable and competent than I thought I was, and I frequently feel Fred's presence guiding me when I am trying to figure things out. I may be overthinking it or oversensitive, but I really feel that those on the other side of the thin veil are reaching out to help us when we need it; we only need to quiet our inner voices and open our eyes to see and hear the messages they leave us. And sometimes, I just need to quit crying so I can hear the inner direction guiding me to the next step.

The Tire
Part 2

It's really remarkable when I stop and look back at how much transpired from the time of Fred's diagnosis to the present which, at this point, is just a few months shy of two years. It seems like a lifetime ago that we were in Australia hiking up the Harbor Bridge and then having his magical sunset birthday dinner on the beach in Fiji. It also seems like it was just yesterday that I heard his voice saying, "Hi, kid, how was your day?" when he would get home or when I would get home from work.

Throughout our marriage, Fred and I divided the household chores. I usually did the laundry, grocery shopping, cooking/dishes, and household finances. I also usually took out the garbage, painted, and took care of the animals. Fred certainly was capable of all of these, would pitch in whenever needed, and often I did not have to ask; he just seemed to know when I needed the help. Since Fred took care of the lawn, planting/pruning trees and bushes, ongoing maintenance of the house and property, and snow/ice removal and management, I didn't have to worry about those things. I tried to be as independent as possible with my chores. I knew how busy he was with work, and it always was in the back of my head that an accident could happen related to his firefighting or lawn/snow business, and I would need to be able to take care of myself.

I have shared about the tire issue shortly after Fred died. I still truly believe that it was a God moment that the very large screw which was clearly embedded in my tire was miraculously gone when I got to the garage. I don't think it was a coincidence or happenstance.

Fred would have gladly showed me how to put air in the tire or change the tire if I had asked, and yes, I should have asked. I always thought I was either too busy or that it just wasn't a good time to learn those skills. Since I have AAA and roadside assistance through my car insurance, I thought I was covered. While I do have a good backup plan, not knowing these simple skills is irresponsible. As a driver, I should know how to do these tasks.

Fast forward to the summer of 2018, almost two years after Fred's death. I began to have a "sensor issue" with my relatively new vehicle. I took care of contacting the dealership and getting my car in for service, which is nothing miraculous. The next day, I got a low tire pressure message on my car. At first I thought it was the sensor again but stopped to check the tire, and indeed, the right passenger tire was a little low. I thankfully had a friend with me who showed me how to put air in the tire. I realize it isn't rocket science, but tires under pressure scare me, and I was always afraid of having a problem if I had to put air into a tire. The low tire message went away, and so I thought it was no longer an issue. I have learned things are rarely as easy as they first seem, and the low tire issue was no different. The next day, as I headed into town, the low tire pressure message returned. Instead of becoming hysterical, I calmly pulled into the local gas station to the air pump and put air into my tire to the correct PSI. I eventually ended up at the tire garage, and they fixed the hole in my tire which was the cause of the low tire pressure readings.

Over the past years, I have learned that "the buck stops here." I can ask for help or hire someone to help me when I can't fix or deal with the issue; however, it is always going to be my responsibility to get the process started. I was so blessed that Fred took care of so much, and I am reminded daily of how lucky I was to have him help me. I also have to admit that I feel guilty that I took him for granted for over thirty-two years. Don't get me wrong, I did appreciate him, and I told him that frequently, but I don't think I really understood the magnitude of his contribution to the marriage until I didn't have him here with me anymore. If I could do one thing over again, it would be to make sure he understood just how much I depended on him and appreciated all he did for me and our sons. I hope he knows that now, somehow, as he looks down from heaven. I share this so that anyone reading this can take heed; please, thank your loved ones for all they do for you!

In addition to the generator, the propane tank, the garage door opener, and the furnace repairs, I also had a leak in the roof. I had to figure out the correct furnace filter, the correct kind of salt for the water softener, and where to get straw for the dog kennel. I realize that none of these are earth-shattering issues. They do seem to compound though; I call it "the drip factor." When there is just one issue to deal with it, it is annoying, but they all seem to hit all at once, or sequentially, and then it begins to feel overwhelming.

Issues arose when Fred was alive, but we either dealt with it together, or often, he would just add it to his list of "things to do" and eventually get it done. It might not have been on my timeline, however. I feel the pressure now that it falls solely on me, and that is scary at times. I think when we feel we are independent it is a facade. That is difficult for me to admit, but it is the truth, and I suppose that the first step in dealing with anything is admitting the issue; no man (or woman) is an island.

I very much dislike being dependent on anyone. It's funny because, all along, I was more dependent on Fred than I realized. He was such a quiet giant at my back and so selfless. He knew how independent I wanted to be, and he allowed me to believe that I was independent. Ha! Fred's death has brought me to my knees and brought me closer to God. I think I wandered away from really understanding how dependent I am for all that I have as well as what I don't have. Understanding that God has provided all I need has given me more good things than I deserve and yet has not given me things all the bad things I deserve has been truly life-changing. He shows me mercy and grace every day, and I am completely dependent on those.

None of us knows what lies ahead, and I think that is a good thing. If I did not have my faith, I would be terrified at what could befall me. Losing Fred was certainly the most difficult thing I have ever been through, but I am sure there will be great difficulties ahead. I have learned that being dependent is OK as long as I face my need for help and understand where I need to direct it, and that is toward

God. It's an odd thing that a tire can teach me that I am not independent and yet I am strong enough to get through the difficulties I will face. God is truly amazing! Step by step, trudging through the Tar Pit. It is sometimes a very dark place, and yet it can be quite enlightening.

We Are All Part of Each Other's Story

As Fred and I stepped onto the path at his diagnosis, we knew that it would be a difficult and painful walk. That was certainly an understatement! As our family, friends, and community learned of our news, we became part of their story, and they became part of ours. Years ago, the tagline, "It takes a village," was coined in reference to raising a child. I think it takes a village as well to get through difficulties in life. In my small Ohio community, in and around Ashland, we have suffered an unusually high number of tragedies. The community has grieved deaths of teenagers in car accidents, seen the loss of life and property in house fires, and lost many to cancer, etc. When the losses come, the community rises to the occasion to take care of the needs of those affected by the tragedy. Those community helpers become "part of the story" of recovery for those that were assisted.

When my Facebook posts began at Fred's diagnosis, it was to give accurate information so we didn't have rumors going around. We knew it would be very difficult to keep all our family and friends up to date in a timely manner, and most were on Facebook. It wasn't what either of us wanted to do—to publicly share such personal information—but it seemed the best way to communicate to the masses. Little did I know how much our story would resonate with others. Soon we began to hear from people far away, people we hadn't seen or heard from in years. We even heard from strangers who were told about us and they asked to become Facebook friends to follow us. We received support from so many and were told many felt solace from us as they watched us, mainly Fred, face death with such dignity and faith.

I have learned that we are all interconnected and intertwined in this world. We sometimes move through our days as if we are an island, and our actions have little influence or effect on others. Perhaps in days of old, when we were not so "plugged in," that may have been truer; however, in the current state of the world, we are all just a click away from connecting literally anywhere in the world. What we find out is that we all, no matter what language we speak or what color our skin is, have the same stories. Stories of joy, of pain, of birth, of death. We all struggle, because of our human frailty, to find meaning to the negative things that happen to us.

People have reached out to me who I had no idea were widows or widowers. Many of these people I knew casually but never really had the opportunity to "know" them. They have shared their stories of loss and pain and resilience and support. They have become part of my story of recovery and finding my way, and I have become part of theirs as they have grown through their ability to share with others. It's really been quite a remarkable experience.

In watching others tell their story and in my daily devotionals, I have been able to appreciate the positive and feel gain in such deep and painful loss. I would have never believed that would be the case. I certainly gave lip service in the past to the whole "silver lining" concept, but I don't think I was ever tested enough to have to believe it. And yet, I can now see the silver lining and gain in my loss. I have never been closer in my walk with God than when I have been brought to my knees in pain and despair. When the only light I can see in the cold and black darkness of the Tar Pit is the light of Christ and the smallness of my life is obvious, it is then that I realize that all my worry and fear do nothing to change things. Think about it; we all carry the self-imposed burdens of life around. We want God to fix things and make life easy, but we want to *be* God so we do not cast our burdens on Him. We carry burdens around, pick up others' burdens, try to shift ours onto others, and the world keeps turning. Each day we are loaded down more and more. When I finally realized that God wants me to only ask Him for help and give Him my burdens and that he will carry me through my difficulties, I found it easier to lay the burdens down and pick up the yoke He offers. He does not say it will be easy, but He does promise to stay at my side. Of course,

I have to make sure I don't run ahead though, and that is a daily challenge for me. Patience and walking slow are not my strong suit.

In the end, God knows what we need before we do. He knows how this all ends for each of us. We think we have "the plan," at least I did. My nature is to plan, make lists, check off things on my list, make new lists, etc. I somehow felt that gave me control. I had a false sense of security—that if I just planned enough, worked enough, it would be enough and I would be "enough." And yet, it never felt like it was "enough." So the viscous cycle of working and doing and planning continued. I am not sure when I thought I was finally going to get off the spinning cycle of planning-doing-planning, but I do know that God had different plans. I admit I hated His plan; it was a bitter and painful pill to swallow. My plan was to have Fred in my life and our children/grandchildren's lives for many more years. We were to grow old together, and I would continue to nag at him about eating better, and he would continue to leave hats, coats, and socks lying around the house to make me crazy. Wow! That was not the plan at all—that was not going to be "the story." Instead, God decided that the plans Fred and I had would be drastically different.

It felt as if the world stopped the day, I realized Fred had a brain tumor, and that was prior to the MRI. The day of the MRI only confirmed the horrible reality that I already knew. All my plans, all Fred's plans, all the work, work, work we always seemed caught up in became so unimportant. The story of our lives would be forever changed.

And so the story came full circle for us. Throughout Fred's fight with "the dragon" of brain cancer, many people shared his story, and as they shared, they became part of our story. The love and support we received from so many were simply remarkable. After Fred died, the family and I were so buoyed up again by love and support.

Many people have continued to add to my story or were part of the story before Fred's diagnosis. I watched those people go before me and deal with trials and adversity, never realizing that they were teaching me through their story. There are so many people who have taught me over the years how to deal with plans that didn't come to fruition.

My maternal grandfather and grandmother divorced when my mom was young, and they both remarried. My grandmother would have another child, divorce, and remarry again. She was a wonderful woman, and I don't know why her marriages weren't successful. It doesn't matter; what does matter is that my mom, my uncle Dick, and aunt Mary were not raised in a traditional family setting and were quite poor, yet they persevered. My parents, and Uncle Dick and Aunt Judy have been married for sixty-plus years and almost sixty years respectively. What an incredible testament!

My grandfather remarried and had another six children, uncles Paul, Steve, Donn, Lee, and Jody, and my aunt Ty. My grandfather was a wonderful man and father, but he did not make much money, particularly for a large family. He lived in Wyoming, so most summer vacations involved a trip to visit him and my aunt and uncles. I watched them grow up with far fewer resources than my brother and I had growing up, and they were happy, hardworking, and very close as siblings. They inspired me to make the best of any circumstances.

Uncle Donn has been a particularly positive influence on me. He is only a year older than me; he is more like a big brother than an uncle. While we didn't grow up close by location, we have always had a special closeness. He is such a sweet and kind and hard-working man. I watched him and my Aunt Pam go through the horror of losing a grandchild and daughter-in-law in a tragic car accident. While they were grieving, they still had to provide strength and support for their son Patrick, and their faith *never* wavered. That blow was more than most families could handle, but there was more to come. Donn continued to work hard despite almost unbearable back pain. Through many years, physicians, and quite a bit of dollar expenditure, it was finally discovered that part of his pain and developing disabilities were actually due to multiple sclerosis. This man who always worked so hard to provide would soon need to come to terms that he could not continue to work. Most people would have become distraught, be angry at God, become bitter, but not my Uncle Donn. This man continues to have the same gentle spirit, kind soul, and deep love of God despite all that has been thrown at him. When I think of someone with "the patience of Job," my Uncle Donn is the first person to come to mind.

The people like my Uncle Donn show us the way, they can't help but to become part of our story. I did not fully comprehend how important those people are who show us the way through adversity and pain and their own Tar Pits. I have written about those who are lighthouses as well. I think we need both kinds of people to help us with our Tar Pit dwelling, our reckoning, our path to find our way out of the Tar Pit, and those people can't help but to become part of our story.

I find great strength in my daily devotional and Bible reading. It is interesting how I look forward to my time with God so much more now that I did when I was younger. This is something from one of my devotional readings:

> When we honestly ask ourselves which person in our lives means the most to us, we often find that it is those who, instead of giving advice, solutions, or cures, have chosen rather to share our pain and touch our wounds with a warm and tender hand. (Henri Nouwen)

These are the people who become integral to our story.

Trees, Flowers, and Birds

As I began jotting down titles for chapters in a book I wanted to write someday, I noticed that many of the titles had to do with trees, flowers, and birds. I have always been drawn into and toward nature. As a child I can remember watching Mutual of Omaha's Wild Kingdom on Sunday nights with my parents and my brother. We traveled every summer on wonderful vacations seeing the country, and often, one of our destinations was a national park or two on our way to visit family who lived out West, or on our way home.

I much preferred to play outside than stay inside as a child. My childhood home was in Jeromesville until sixth grade. My family then moved outside Hayesville. This gave me ample space and opportunity to get out and enjoy nature, even if, some days, it was raking what seemed to be an endless supply of leaves in the fall. Whether it was collecting fireflies or caterpillars or garter snakes, I enjoyed getting up close and personal with God's creations. I am not sure my parents always appreciated my love of nature when I brought nature into the house. However, the time I rescued the baby owl, they did think it was pretty cool.

In Jeromesville, we had a pear tree and sour cherry tree in our backyard as well as a rather large grape arbor, and Mom had a rose garden. I still can smell the fresh horseradish Dad would dig up and grind into horseradish that would be stored in jars in the refrigerator. My brother and I spent a great deal of time in trees during the summer. We picked cherries or pears in the summer. We climbed the trees around town or later in our woods when we moved out in the country. Sometimes we climbed the mulberry tree across from our property in Jeromesville so we could shake the berries onto a sheet and eat them.

We had a Purple Martin house on our property in Jeromesville. Mom and Dad taught us that they were wonderful birds which helped control insects. Controlling the mosquitoes certainly made for more comfortable evenings playing outside. The birds also helped to control other insects, which made for healthier fruit crops around our house. Oh, and then there were the fruit bats! I like bats and was always fascinated by them flying around in the evening eating insects. My brother, however, hated bats. I suppose I should ask him if he still does, but suffice it to say, that was one of his phobias growing up. I quickly discovered that locking my brother out of the house in the evening when he went out to burn the trash when the bats were out was a way to mess with him. Eventually, I would have to let him in, and I would pay for my decision. For some reason though, I continued to mess with him... Siblings!

When Fred and I started dating, and then as we learned what interests we had in common, we found we both loved being outdoors, hiking, gardening, and travel. At each house we lived in, we planted trees, bushes, flowers, and had a garden. When we bought our property and built our house, we had a blank canvas to plant and landscape. We found great joy in planting a variety of items. Fred, with the help of Nicolaus as a young child, planted hundreds of trees. As Christopher grew, he too learned to plan and plant landscaping projects. Both of our sons today still enjoy doing projects as they were taught by their dad.

I do have to laugh, though; you know what they say about karma. Sometimes I wanted things planted in certain locations that Fred wasn't particularly thrilled about. Sometimes he would convince me I was wrong, and sometimes, he would just give in and plant what I wanted in the location I requested. Often, it worked out fine, sometimes, it did not. After Fred died and I began mowing our quite large yard, I started mowing around all the plantings from twenty-five-plus years. Hum...to say some of my choices were not the best is an understatement. Fred truly was patient as he mowed around things that were inconveniently placed. I smile and actually laugh out loud somedays as I mow. I also have cut down or moved some of the plantings. I guess it's all about perspective.

Trees are interesting. There are so many types, and they need certain conditions to thrive. They need stress as they grow to be able to become strong and put down deep roots. Trees also are able to keep growing even when pruned, have limbs cut off, or are otherwise injured. Flowers are more fragile and less forgiving. Trees and flowers add beauty and enrich our lives and have a great deal to teach if we stop and observe.

There is a maple tree in my far backyard. Fred and one of the boys planted it years ago. It grew tall and straight and was doing quite well. One day, Fred decided he would burn the brush pile in the backyard. The fire turned into quite a conflagration, and though neither of us expected the flames would reach that maple tree, they did indeed. That poor tree took quite a bit of "stress" from the intense heat as well as the sparks that made their way to the leaves and bark. We both were sure the tree was going to die; it looked like it was dying the rest of that summer and into the fall. We talked about cutting it down before the high winter winds came and blew it over. In the end, the tree didn't get cut down, and to this day, it is still standing, and it is alive. One side of it is scarred from the fire, and some of the limbs don't produce as many leaves as the limbs that faced away from the fire. The point is, though, that tree, despite tremendous stress and "pain," has survived. I can see that tree looming tall in my backyard from my house. When I walk the dog in the backyard, I see the scars, and I am reminded that intense stress and pain may change us and wound us, but it doesn't have to ruin us. Oddly, that tree is one of the most beautiful trees on my property to me.

I was generally the flower gardener between Fred and I. He helped haul dirt for my flower beds or flower pots. He would help me water, but generally, I was the one who picked out the flowers, planted them, and tended to them all season. He loved the flowers, and we spent as much time as we could on the patio enjoying the flowers and watching the butterflies, bees, and hummingbirds enjoying them as well. The summer before Fred died was particularly special for enjoying the flowers and the patio. He was so tired most of the time that just sitting was all the energy he could muster once he got outside. It forced me to sit more often with him than flit and flutter around, and we simply enjoyed the sights, smells, and sounds. Those times were such a gift. I can almost hear him when I sit on the patio.

Many flowers aren't as forgiving as trees, however—too much water, they die; too little water, they die; too hot, many of them shrivel up; too little sun, they are stunted. Flowers require more time, attention, patience, and "love." Flowers need tended to if they are to thrive. Some flowers, such as peonies, are dependent on ants to help them bloom and bring forth their beauty. I think people are a lot like flowers. People need the right environment to grow and thrive. It is a mixture of sun, shade, water (the right amount), temperature, and other influences such as birds, bees, and butterflies that make flowers truly beautiful. Flowers can't just be planted and left alone—just like people. When we are grieving, we have the same needs as flowers sometimes though we don't recognize that in ourselves or in others. When we ignore our needs or those around us, we can quickly shrivel just like tender flowers.

And then there are the birds. I spend quite a bit of time bird watching, feeding the birds, and listening to the birds. I look forward to the robins in late winter returning. Seeing the first bluebirds of the season never ceases to make me smile. Watching the sparrows eat the Rose of Sharon flowers fascinates me. I love to see the humming-birds at my feeders and enjoying the flowers I plant to try and attract them. My small pond is a mecca for the birds in the winter as well as throughout spring, summer, and fall.

I like all my birds; the cardinals are extra special though. Fred's mom told me years ago that cardinals were her favorite birds because they mated for life. She also told me that it is believed that, when a cardinal visits, it is a visitor from heaven.

I have several bird feeders, so I have many birds that are con-stantly flying in and out. I watch my birds from my back windows, and they entertain me when I am in the kitchen, especially when doing the dishes. (Yes, I still hand wash my dishes.) After Fred died, it was sometimes difficult to cook and eat, and often, my meals would be something very simple. I usually didn't have many dishes to wash and didn't spend much time at the kitchen sink.

One day, I decided I was going to make an egg, spinach, and potato frittata. I spent time preparing and cooking the potatoes and then added the spinach and eggs and topped it all with cheese. Then I put it in the oven. Of course, this all took much more time than a container of yogurt, my "go to" breakfast or peanut butter. As I started the preparation, I noticed a male cardinal in the bush outside the kitchen window. There was no female to be found. That cardinal stayed in the bush the entire time I was preparing ingredients, cooking the frittata, and even while I stood at the sink eating it. All in all, close to an hour. I finished eating, looked away for a split second, and the cardinal was gone.

This occurred about the time I began to finally climb out of the depths of despair. I had felt deeply entrenched in the Tar Pit for months, and it was difficult to appreciate a sunny day or have any appetite or have any desire to cook anything. That cardinal showed up and kept me company throughout the whole process. It hasn't happened since then. I frequently have cardinals, and sometimes I have pairs outside the bedroom window in my trees. Sometimes I just have a male, but I haven't had one linger for that long outside my kitchen window since that day.

Thankfully, we humans aren't only as fragile as flowers; we also have the resiliency of trees within us. We also have the ability to "show up" for others like a certain cardinal did for me months ago. We are such complex creatures that only a loving and all-knowing God could create. I feel blessed that, at a young age, my parents imparted a love for, and then a knowledge of, nature. I feel lucky that I found a partner who appreciated nature with me and taught me even more. I am refreshed daily as I am surrounded by nature, a gift from God. It is nature that helps to sustain me on the sad days and makes me smile on those days when I can simply take in the sights, sounds, and smells.

The Tar Pit at Year Two

I am amazed that, as I write this, the second anniversary of Fred's death is looming. I cannot believe how fast and yet how slow it has gone. It's mind boggling at what has taken place in two years, how things have changed, how far I have come in my path through the Tar Pit, and…how far I have yet to go.

My goal when I started writing was to put my thoughts and feelings into words. Check—that goal has been completed. As Fred and I started walking on the cancer path in May of 2016, we discussed that we would share our walk publicly to reduce the rumor mill and get the facts out to everyone. We also wanted to share our faith with others and that, despite the most devastating news and circumstances, God is good, and He sustains us if we only ask and receive. Fred showed us such grace and strength even as his body weakened and as death loomed.

At times like this, I wish I could type as fast as my mind comes up with thoughts and ideas. I do some of my best thinking when walking and working outside, but it's hard to write or even dictate when holding a shovel, spade, or the garden hose, or when weeding. I have ideas when I am "doing," and then have to try to remember what I wanted to write when I have time to collect my thoughts again. I have such respect for the great writers through the centuries and how they gathered their thoughts into literary works of art!

Many people have given me sage advice regarding their path through the Tar Pit. What I hear consistently is "Karin, you never really get out of the Tar Pit." When I first heard that, I was disheartened. "My plan" was to forge ahead on the path through the dark and sticky tar and come out on the other side feeling healed and whole. Once again, I am reminded that completion of my plans is not always possible, and they do not always turn out as hoped. I am learning to redirect my thinking and become more accepting of the current situation. I did not say, however, that I was "good" at that yet; I am still in the learning phase.

Crying is something I do not like to do. For one thing, it's not a "pretty cry," and yes, that's called being vain, but it's the truth. A second reason I do not like to cry is that I almost always end up with a headache when done crying. The third reason, I feel weak and vulnerable when crying, and I truly do not like that feeling at all. Ah… there's the key, realizing I cannot get successfully through the Tar Pit without others and I cannot "do" life without God. While feeling the need to be strong, I am reminded daily as I'm brought to my knees before God that I can do nothing without Him. Often, His help arrives in the form of other Tar Pit dwellers who are on their own path through the dark and sticky tar.

As I reflect back on the past two years since Fred's death, my scars reveal the work of trudging through the Tar Pit. Scars are interesting things. They reflect outwardly the inner wounds through which we have suffered. At first blush, many times, we think of scars as ugly and something to be hidden. When contemplating the meaning of scars, I now think of them as beautiful. Scars tell a story of struggle, of a battle, of victory. Almost all of us have a scar from something—from a surgery, from an accident, from a burn, and the list goes on. When the injury first occurred which caused the scar, the pain was sharp and sometimes almost unbearable. As time went by, the pain eased, the scar became less raised and visible; it became part of the outer landscape of our skin. Running our fingers over the scar reminds us of the injury and the story behind it. In time, the memory of what caused the scar may remind us how we survived the injury, or maybe it was a great story that makes us smile from a childhood adventure. I must admit though, sometimes feeling the scar brings back the memory of the pain experienced.

Just like the tree in my backyard which was scarred from burning in our "great conflagration" but survived, I too am surviving. I will be forever changed from losing Fred. But just like that tree which doesn't look as beautiful as it once did and is still growing, I too can thrive. I know I will never be the same though. I am trying to learn to accept that fact, however difficult it might be to face. I am learning to be a little more forgiving of myself and others. I've learned that while I still really do not like to cry, sometimes I just have to get it out so I can move through my day and the Tar Pit. Just as running my finger over scars from a surgery or an injury is a reminder of a past experience, I am learning to allow my emotional scar be present as simply part of me, but not be the thing that defines me. Some days the sadness and the scars still overwhelm me and I become too frustrated with myself. I want all the pain to be gone but the realization exists that it may never happen; it might lessen, but mostly likely it will never be gone.

My hope as I ended "year two" without Fred is that I would begin to feel "normal" again; after all, I have been through all "the firsts" and now the "seconds." I am finding out that isn't the way this works. Many who miss Fred have gone on with their lives, and rightly so. If we carried the deep pain of loss and every time a person we cared about died, we would be crushed with grief. The difference is this; the pain felt by the immediate survivor, in this case me, is a pain that carries on forever. I had hoped I would learn my new normal and adapt. While I am adapting, I cannot seem to learn the "new normal," as it still doesn't feel normal, and I don't know when, or if, it ever will again.

As I spend more time in my daily devotional time with God, I am learning that the here and now is just a blink of an eye. Learning that seemingly important things, situations, people, etc. are fleeting and even bad situations will come to an end. Eternity is a much more important thing to focus on, for it truly is the only thing that is forever.

Every time I take communion at church and am kneeling at the rail, I ask God to help me remember that things are not really about me. While I believe that to be true, as a sinner and as a human, I am naturally drawn to believe that life is about me. When we feel the world is about "us," that is when we take things personally, and we begin to feel our hurt is worse than everyone else's. We begin to wallow in self-pity when things don't go our way. God didn't put us on this earth so we would have a wonderful time and always be happy. God put us on this earth with the sole purpose of having a relationship with us, end of story. If we believe it is about us, we have the story all wrong. In developing a relationship with God, we find true happiness and joy despite all the difficulty and the Tar Pit that surrounds us. The relationship we have with God, through Jesus Christ, is *the* only thing that matters, for that is what brings us to eternity in heaven with our Father and all those who go before us through the thin veil.

I have to remember that Fred was a gift to me and our family and to all who loved him; he was not "mine." He was a child of God, and he has returned to his Holy Father. We each have an earthly father, but we all have only one Holy Father. I was blessed with a marvelous gift for over thirty-two years. I continue to receive that gift daily through our sons, their wives, our granddaughters, and the family and friends I gained as mine when we married. I think the return on the investment was astronomical.

Through the gift of my relationship with Fred, I am also blessed to know true, accepting, and deep love. We had the kind of love that was rare, and I didn't understand how many people saw that in our relationship until Fred was diagnosed and people began sharing stories of watching us throughout the years. What a gift! Because of knowing love like that I am able to walk the path through the Tar Pit.

I am not a particularly good swimmer, but I am adequate. (Except for a time in Hawaii when I am grateful Christopher was much more adequate than I was, but that is for another book.) I don't know a great deal about long-distance swimming; however, I see the special coating the swimmers apply when swimming long distances, particularly in cold water. They are preparing for the long and steady pace, not a sprint. That is how I liken the path through the Tar Pit. If we are to successfully navigate the pit, we have to prepare for the long haul just as a distance swimmer readies him or herself. The coating a swimmer applies is like those we surround ourselves with, words we speak to ourselves, devotional readings, and other things that sustain us. These relationships and words are there to help us through the cold and dark tar pit. It takes so much effort some days to simply get out of bed. I cannot imagine having to do it without the words of encouragement that sustain me.

We have had an unusually hot summer this year, and September has started out very hot. I do not like the hot and humid weather at all and can be rather verbal about my distain for the heat a.k.a. whiny! It's interesting though, I still do enjoy the hot weather, at least parts of it. When I am out for my daily walk, I like watching the tar bubbles on the road. As a kid, I can remember my friends and I would go out into the alleys in Jeromesville in the summer heat and pop the tar bubbles. It was always fun to see how many big bubbles we could find and how far into the air the fluid inside the bubble would rise when we popped the bubble. I've thought a great deal about those bubbles and the fact that they only form when the tar is under stress, in this case, heat. My brother has told me for years that it was his role as my big brother to "shape me" and that coal only becomes a diamond under pressure. That was his reasoning for picking on me growing up. (I laugh now because I think growing up with an older brother prepared me for raising two sons and a husband.) Tar bubbles and older sibling can teach us a great deal—that only when we are stretched and stressed and placed under pressure do we really understand what we can become. Easy seems so much better; however, hard and difficult is really what shapes and forms our character. I am certainly not the same person now that I was prior to Fred's diagnosis and subsequent death. I have changed; I hope I have become a more patient and compassionate person, and I know my faith has deepened and been strengthened.

As I look ahead to the next part of my life, stepping near the edge of the Tar Pit is scary. Being in the pit is awful, but as I've written before, it is a comfortable rut. The thing about a rut is that you have an idea of what to expect. Admittedly, I am what is frequently referred to as "a control freak." I don't wear that as a positive part of my character. It makes having things happen unexpectedly feel very uncomfortable. I am a planner, not just for plan A but usually plan B and C. None of the last two years have gone as planned.

I don't know what the future holds, and that's probably good. It's doubtful that I've seen the end of heartbreak. The reality of life is that it's difficult, painful, and filled with sadness and disappointment at times. It also is filled with joy, wonder, and unanticipated and unexpected delights. Learning to be open to the unexpected is a key element to being happy as well as being able to use good times to sustain us through the bad.

And finally, learning to find "me" again is hard, and I must admit, it hasn't been very enjoyable, but today, I was reminded by a high school teacher that there was a "me" before there was an "us." We reflected back on his early years as an educator and mine as a high school student at Hillsdale High School. He knew Fred had died but hadn't seen me since then and expressed his condolences. I told him I was on the path through the Tar Pit and I was writing a book. He gave me encouragement and said he thought it would go well as he remembered me as a good student. It was odd but felt comforting to have a glimmer of "me" before there was an "us." Maybe this Tar Pit dweller is learning to get to shore and gain sure footing, even if I never get completely out of the tar.

Making the Decision to Thrive

Shortly after Fred died, I had a conversation with one of my nephews, Joshua. He asked how I was doing, and I told him, "OK." I chose OK as an answer to that question for months. I didn't feel good or great, and sometimes I didn't feel OK, but I wanted to be that way. As the saying goes, "Fake it until you make it." Dad Rogers used to say, "Never let on, just carrying on." All those sayings seem trite, but I hung on those words early on in the Tar Pit because I did not want to spend my time moping around and feeling sorry for myself. I worried that if I let myself spiral too deep in self-pity, I would never get my head above the tar again.

Misery does love company, but what I have found over the years is that putting a bunch of miserable people in the company of each other does not make them feel better. In the end, the whole group of people become more despondent the more they commiserate about their misery. The last thing I wanted to do was to feel more despondent.

Joshua shared with me that he looked up to me and how strong I always seemed to him. His maternal grandmother had lost her first husband when she was younger than me, and she eventually remarried years later but lost that husband too. He talked about how strong he thought she was, and he felt I was that strong as well. He told me he could see me being happy and full of life despite the loss of his beloved Uncle Fred. I am not sure Joshua knows how much he inspired me during those early weeks/months after Fred's death. It was all I could do to put one foot in front of the other, and I was told by Joshua that he could envision me happy and thriving. I am not sure I believed him, but I certainly wanted to feel happy and thrive at some point again.

Part of learning to thrive again is making the conscious decision to be happy or at least to not be sad. It seems a simple concept, but sometimes, the simple concept is difficult to put into practice. The dark black cloud of grieving hung over me daily and throughout the many long and sleepless nights. Lack of sleep makes the ability to deal with minor stresses difficult and major stresses seem almost insurmountable. It was hard to think of thriving and being happy when I couldn't even get a good night's sleep.

Years ago, I was given a book by a close friend and the companion journal for tracking gratitude. I read the book and attempted to keep up on the gratitude journal daily. That lasted for about a month and then journaling stopped. I decided I needed to put a plan into action if I was going to make the decision to be happy come to fruition. I thought about the gratitude journal I started years prior.

Sometimes before we can be happy, we have to at least become "less sad feeling." That idea seemed like something I could more easily accomplish vs. feeling happy, and so I began with that as my focus. I started reading the book *Jesus Calling* by Sarah Young shortly after Fred died. It is set up for a daily reading January 1 to December 31. On January 1, 2017, I started the book from the beginning and each night wrote something I was grateful for on that day's message. Some days I struggled to find something I was grateful for; "a warm bed" was all I could muster some days, and other days, I wrote "family" or "comfort food." I smile now as I think of myself sitting trying to come up with something to write. I read my gratitude notes periodically as reminder of how far I have come and how far I have to go on the path through the Tar Pit. It keeps me grounded; it keeps me humble when I think I am farther along than I actually am. It reminds me that every day, even in great sorrow and despair, I have something for which to be grateful.

Being grateful and choosing to thrive isn't the same as just being happy. I am reminded of Paul and his struggles as he suffered; he was beaten, shipwrecked, whipped, etc. He wrote of his learning to be satisfied and grateful even as he suffered in prison and as he faced his imminent death in Rome. I am sure he wasn't necessarily happy, but he still was thriving, and he was content as he shared the message of Christ while sitting in prison.

I found as I made the conscious decision to not be as sad with the goal of eventually being happy, it was easier to answer "OK" and believe it when people asked how I was doing. As "OK" flowed more easily, I also found my days seemed a little brighter. I certainly had sadness creep in and tears flow, but I began to feel like I was going to be OK. I could hear Dad Rogers saying, "Never let on. Just carry on."

As time went by, when people asked how I was doing, I began to say, "I am well." It was interesting to see the look on faces when I responded that way instead of "OK." I often received a smile and sometimes a pause followed by something like, "Wow, that's good to hear," or, "So glad to hear that." Misery may love company, but I think not being sad draws people toward us. We generally are drawn to light, and when we work toward not being sad, it brightens our world as well as the world of those around us. Part of the sadness we feel when we are grieving is because we are lonely. Pulling people toward us helps to fight the loneliness. There is a difference however between the companionship we receive from family and friends and the intimacy we have with our spouse or significant other.

I was reluctant to answer "good" when asked how I was doing as the months went by for fear that maybe some days I wouldn't feel "good" and people would think I was crazy as I vacillated back and forth. Eventually, I made the decision that I wanted to feel good despite feeling the hole still so big in my heart. Then began the conscious decision to answer "good" on those days I felt strong and "well" on those days when things were a little more difficult for me. I found people were more apt to stop and talk to me about things such as how they were doing or share special memories of Fred or simply offer me their best wishes. At the end of these interactions, I almost always felt better, further adding to the feeling of "good."

In no way do I mean to minimize the deep and sorrowful pain felt with the loss of a loved one. Life is never the same when we lose someone we love, whether it be a loss from death, from divorce, or the end of a relationship. When we love deeply and completely, we will never be the same after we lose that person. I do believe, though, that walking around in continued sadness doesn't honor the relationship or the person we have lost. If we feel the loss, we generally felt joy when we had that person with us. Making the conscious decision to "not be sad" and focus on simple things to be grateful for each day can go a long way in helping us eventually find joy in our lives.

Learning to thrive again after a loss is an easy thing to say, but it isn't an easy thing to accomplish. It isn't impossible though. If Paul could learn to be content despite all his suffering, we certainly can strive for contentment and joy as well. It isn't a sign that we didn't love or don't miss our loved one; it is a tribute to the loved one that we want to find joy again.

Choosing to Leave the Path and Start on the Next Journey

The title of this book is *Walking the Tar Pit*. I have previously explained that I didn't call the time we dealt with Fred's cancer diagnosis and eventual death as a "journey." Many refer to their dealing with cancer as a journey, and that certainly is a way to describe it, though I think of journeys as an adventure to look forward to and that should be fun. Fred and I loved to travel, and we were blessed to go on wonderful journeys. There was nothing about the cancer path that was fun nor did we look forward to any part of it. However, I do think we made the best of the time we had left by spending quality time together, laughing, crying, and sharing our innermost thoughts and feelings with each other, knowing death was to come.

I can honestly say I was blessed through part of this experience on the path because I felt the love and support from so many in my family and community. I saw God hold me up when my knees buckled under me. When I felt I could not take one more step and during times I could barely breathe through the pain and grief, God has been by my side.

Walking on the path through the Tar Pit has allowed me to connect with people at a level that I never would have been able to do if not for this experience. When a patient, patient's family, a friend, or a casual stranger discusses with me their deep grief, I can look them in the eye and tell them "I understand." I do not mean I know exactly how they feel for everyone's walk on the path through the Tar Pit is different, but I do understand. As I have said before, when fellow Tar Pit dwellers look at each other, they make a connection that others cannot make.

I realize that there comes a decision time where I must choose to leave "the path" and head out on my journey through life again or stay stuck walking on this path. "The Tar Pit" will always be part of my journey; I don't think any of us ever completely leave the Tar Pit. We swim, trudge, and walk through it; we hang out on the shore with our feet in it; we get dragged back in by a big wave of tar, but I finally realize that "the path" can be separated from "the Tar Pit."

The decision to venture out as Karin, not the poor widow lady, is scary and exciting. It's been a long time since I graduated as a seventeen-year-old from my alma mater, Hillsdale High School (HHS). I ventured out to college, by myself, not knowing anyone. I left for Kent State on my big adventure, scared to death but excited and looking forward to the future, even though it was full of uncertainty. When I think about the life skills I have now compared to then, I certainly should be able to do at least as well. I stayed safe and I didn't get arrested for any bad decisions. I made my way to a successful profession and career. I hope this fifty-six-year-old can do the same.

I have never made Baked Alaska, but I have tasted it a few times. It isn't my favorite dessert, but I do like it. What does Baked Alaska have to do with grief, walking the path, and being in the Tar Pit? It seems to me that Baked Alaska is an enigma or a paradox. It is a blend of ice cream inside of a cake that is then covered with a meringue and then is baked until brown. It seems amazing that the ice cream can stay firm and yet the meringue can brown in the oven. Some things are simply beyond my understanding I suppose. The good news is that for Baked Alaska to be tasty, it does not require my understanding or skill. The experience of eating Baked Alaska only requires me to believe it will be tasty when I eat it, and I leave it up to someone more skilled than me to create it.

Making the decision to leave the path and head out on my next journey is like the Baked Alaska experience. I do not have to create the journey or understand how it will happen, I simply have to have faith that "Someone," and as it relates to life, God, will create the experience for me that He wants. I am to participate in the journey just like ordering and eating Baked Alaska. For me, and I imagine many others, this leap of faith is a difficult one. Having to be in control of a situation, wanting to know all the answers, and feeling like we have to be the ones leading the journey are all normal human feelings. Some of us are more control freaks than others, but I think all of us like to feel like we control somethings in our life.

When our world is turned upside down with a devastating loss, be it the loss of a job, a child, a spouse, etc., it is unsettling. We feel out of control. The path is set before us, and it is scary, dark and difficult. This is all part of the human condition. We were not meant to walk the path alone. My deep faith in God tells me that even when we are physically alone and feel full of despair, God is always with us, but we must be willing to seek Him and ask for help. He is always standing near us; we just have to reach out and hold His hand. I felt His hand so many times in the days since Fred died, when I was physically alone but asked for His presence to be with me. I simply could not have gone on without my hand in God's hand each day.

I want very much to put the path and the Tar Pit far behind me. It would be much less painful to not have the sadness engulf me when I least expect it. It would be less painful to walk in the morning and see a beautiful sunrise and not remember how much Fred looked forward to his sunrise view on his way to Hillsdale during the summers he worked as a custodian. I would like to not cry when I still see certain people that Fred loved to tease and joke around with every time they were together. And oh…the songs, how certain songs will always stop me in my tracks and bring me to tears as well as a card or letter I periodically find with Fred's handwriting.

Realistically though, I don't think I can ever put the loss so far behind me that I won't be affected by it. I am learning to live on a parallel line, though, as I step off the path onto the next journey just like I left HHS and headed off to college. I could not stay a seventeen-year-old forever. I could choose to stay on the path, but I don't think that's a good option. It wastes what life I have left on this earth, and we are supposed to use our days productively to do God's will. I think His will is learning to share ourselves with others as we head on the journey to our ultimate final destination. Sometimes we are on a path for a while, but venturing out on the next journey is an option I now can see as a realistic and maybe I will stop for a Baked Alaska on the way forward.

Devotionals and Inspirational Verses

I started writing short stories and poetry when I was in late elementary school and throughout junior high, and at the same time, I began to collect verses and poems that were inspirational and have amassed quite a collection over the years. Once Fred was diagnosed with brain cancer, I found the words that inspired me to be different from what "spoke" to me when I was younger. It wasn't so much about "being a better me," which was the focus of my writings in my formative years. From Fred's diagnosis and continuing since his death and beyond, it has been about finding the strength to move on the path through the Tar Pit. I wanted to include some of those readings in this book with the hope that they help others. It should come as no surprise that many of the sayings and verses are faith based.

Scriptures

The Lord himself goes before you and will be with you; he will never leave you nor forsake you. Do not be afraid; do not be discouraged. (Deuteronomy 31:8)

Have I not commanded you? Be strong and courageous. Do not be terrified; do not be discouraged, for the Lord your God will be with you wherever you go. (Joshua 1:9)

Thou has enlarged me when I was in distress. (Psalm 4:1)

How long; O Lord? Will you forget me forever? How long will you hide your face from me? How long must I wrestle with my thoughts and every day have sorrow in my heart? How long will my enemy triumph over me? Look on me and answer, O Lord my God. Give light to my eyes, or I will sleep in death; my enemy will say, 'I have overcome him'. And my foes will rejoice when I fall. But I trust in your unfailing love; my heart rejoices in your salvation, I will sing to the Lord, for he has been good to me. (Psalm 13:1–6)

Therefore my heart is glad and my tongue rejoices; my body also will rest secure, because you will not abandon me to the grave, nor will you let your Holy One see decay. You have made known to me the path of life; you will fill me with joy in your presence, with eternal pleasures at your right hand. (Psalm 16: 9–11)

I love you, O Lord, my strength. The Lord is my rock, my fortress and my deliverer; my God is my rock, in whom I take refuge. He is my shield and the horn of my salvation, my stronghold. I call to the Lord, who is worthy of praise, and I am saved from my enemies. The cords of death entangled me; the torrents of destruction overwhelmed me. The cords of the grave coiled around me; the snares of death confronted me. In my distress I called to the Lord; I cried to me God for help. From his temple he heard me voice; my cry came before him, into his ears… He reached down from on high and took hold of me; he drew me out of deep waters. (Psalm 18:1–6, 16)

Weeping may stay for the night, but rejoicing comes in the morning. (Psalm 30:5)

I waited patiently for the Lord; he turned to me and heard my cry. He lifted me out of the slimy pit, out of the mud and the mire; he set my feet on a rock and gave me a firm place to stand. (Psalm 40: 1–3)

When I am afraid, I will trust you. (Psalm 56:3)

O Lord, The God who saves me, day and night I cry out before you. May my prayer come before you; turn your ear to my cry. For my soul is full of trouble and my life draws near the grave. I am counted among those who go down to the pit; I am like a man without strength. I am set apart with the dead, like the slain who lie in the grave, whom you remember no more, who are cut off from your care. You have put me in the lowest pit, in the darkest depths. Your wrath lies heavily upon me; you have overwhelmed me with all your waves. You have taken from me my closest friends and have made me repulsive to them. I am confined and cannot escape; my eyes are dim with grief. I call to you, O Lord, every day; I spread out my hands to you. Do you show your works to the dead? Do those who are dead rise up and praise you? Is your love declared in the grave, your faithfulness in destruction? Are your wonders known in the places of darkness, or your righteous deeds in the land of oblivion? But I cry to you for help, O Lord; in the morning my prayer comes before you. Why, O Lord, do you reject me and hide your face from me? … You have taken my companions and loved

ones from me; the darkness is my closest friend.
(Psalm 88:1–14, 18)

*This Psalm, though full of despair allowed me to deeply share my pain with God at my lowest point in the Tar Pit. It shows that when there is no relief in sight, in this instance, Fred's death, God understands even our deepest misery.

Your word is a lamp to my feet and a light
for my path. (Psalm 119: 105)

I lift up my eyes to the mountains, where does my help come from? My help comes from the Lord, the Maker of heaven and earth." (Psalm 121:1–2)

Answer me quickly, O Lord; my spirit fails. Do not hide your face from me or I will be like those who go down to the pit. Let the morning bring me word of your unfailing word love, for I have put me trust in you. Show me the way I should go, for to you I lift up my soul. (Psalm 143:7–8)

Trust in the Lord with all your heart, and lean not on your own understanding; in all your ways acknowledge him, and he will make your paths straight. (Proverbs 3:5–6)

Surely God is my salvation; I will trust and not be afraid. The Lord, the Lord, is my strength and song; he has become my salvation. (Isaiah 12:2)

But those that hope in the Lord will renew their strength. They will soar on wings like eagles; they will run and not grow weary, they will walk and not be faint. (Isaiah 40:31)

So do not fear, for I am with you; do not be discouraged, for I am your God. I will strengthen you and help you. I will uphold you with my righteous hand. (Isaiah 41:10)

For I am the Lord, your God, who takes hold of your right hand and says to you, Do not fear; I will help you. (Isaiah 41:13)

When you pass through the waters, I will be with you; and when you pass through the rivers, they will not sweep over you. When you walk through the fire, you will not be burned; the flames will not set you ablaze. For I am the Lord, your God, the Holy One of Israel, your Savior. (Isaiah 43:2)

Even to your old age and gray hairs I am he, I am he who will sustain you. I have made you and I will carry you. I will sustain you and rescue you. (Isaiah 46:4)

As the heavens are higher than the earth, so are my ways higher than ways and my thoughts than your thoughts. (Isaiah 55:9)

But blessed is the man who trusts in the Lord, whose confidence is in him. (Jeremiah 17:7)

I called on your name, O Lord, from the depths of the pit. You heard my plea: "Do not close your ears to my cry for relief." You came near when I called you, and you said, "Do not fear." (Lamentations 3:55–57)

In my distress I called to the Lord, and he answered me. From the depths of the grave I called for help, and you listened to my cry. You hurled me into the deep, into the very heart of the seas, and the currents swirled about me; all your waves and breakers swept over me. I said 'I have been banished from your sight; yet I will look again toward your holy temple. The engulfing waters threatened me, the deep surrounded me; seaweed was wrapped around my head. To the roots of the mountains I sank down; the earth beneath barred me in forever. But you brought my life up from the pit, O Lord my God.' (Jonah 2:1–6)

But for you who revere my name, the sun of righteousness will rise with healing in its wings. And you will go out and leap like calves released from the stall. (Malachi 4:2)

Therefore I tell you, do not worry about your life, what you will eat or drink; or about your body, what you will wear. Is not life more important than food, and the body more import-ant than clothes? Look at the birds of the air; they do not sow or reap or store away in barns, and yet your heavenly Father feeds them. Are you not much more valuable than they? Who of you by worrying can add a single hour to his life? And why do you worry about clothes? See how the lilies of the field grow. They do not labor or spin. Yet I tell you that not even Solomon in all his splendor was dressed like one of these. If that is how God clothes the grass of the field, which is here today and tomorrow is thrown into the fire, will he not much more clothe you, O you of little faith? So, do not worry, saying, 'What shall we eat?' or 'What shall we drink?' or 'What shall we wear?' For the pagans run after all these things, and your heavenly Father knows that you need them. But seek first his kingdom and his righteousness, and all these things will be given to you as well. Therefore, do not worry about tomorrow, for tomorrow will worry about itself. Each day has enough trouble of its own. (Matthew 6:25–34)

For God so loved the world that he gave his one and only Son, that whoever believes in him shall not perish but have eternal life. (John 3:16)

Do not let your hearts be troubled. Trust in God, trust also in me. In my Father's house are many rooms; if it were not so, I would have told you. I am going there to prepare a place for you. And if I go to prepare a place for you, I will come back and take you to be with me that you also may be where I am. You know the way to the place where I am going. Thomas said to him, 'Lord, we don't know where you are going, so how can we know the way?' Jesus answered I am the way and the truth and the life. No one comes to the Father except through me. (John 14:1–6)

Peace I leave with you; my peace I give to you. I do not give as the world gives. Do not let your hearts be troubled and do not be afraid. (John 14:27)

I have told you these things, so that in me you may have peace. In this world you will have trouble. But take heart! I have overcome the world. (John 16:33)

No, in all these things we are more than conquerors through him who loved us. For I am convinced that neither death nor life, neither angels nor demons, neither the present nor the future, nor any powers, neither height nor depth, nor anything else in all creation, will be able to separate us from the love of God that is in Christ Jesus our Lord. (Romans 8: 37–39)

Praise be to God and Father of our Lord Jesus Christ, the Father of compassion and the God of all comfort, who comforts us in all our troubles, so that we can comfort those in in any trouble with the comfort we ourselves have received from God. (2 Corinthians 1:3–4)

But he said to me 'My grace is sufficient for you, for my power is made perfect in weakness.' Therefore, I will boast all the more gladly about my weaknesses, so that Christ's power may rest on me. That is why, for Christ's sake, I delight in weaknesses, in insults, in hardships, in persecutions, in difficulties. For when I am weak, then I am strong. (2 Corinthians 12:9–10)

Finally, be strong in the Lord and in His mighty power. (Ephesians 6:10)

Rejoice in the Lord always. I will say it again: Rejoice! Let your gentleness be evident to all. The Lord is near. Do not be anxious about anything, but in everything, by prayer and petition, with thanksgiving, present your requests to God. And the peace of God, which transcends all understanding, will guard your hearts and your minds in Christ Jesus. (Philippians 4:4–7)

For I have learned to be content whatever the circumstances. I know what it is to be
in need, and I know what it is to have plenty. I
have learned the secret of being content in any
and every situation, whether well fed or hungry,
whether living in plenty or in want. I can do
everything through him who gives me strength.
(Philippians 4:11–13)

Now faith is being sure of what we hope for
and certain of what we do not see. (Hebrews 11:1)

The entire eleventh chapter of Hebrews is one I find comfort in
reading. The first verse is the one I have committed to memory, and
I have I on my wall in my dining room.

Consider it pure joy, my brothers and sisters,
whenever you face trials of many kinds, because
you know that the testing of your faith produces
perseverance. Let perseverance finish its work so
that you may be mature and complete, not lack-
ing anything… Blessed is the one who perseveres
under trial because, having stood the test, that person will receive the crown of life that the Lord has
promised to those who love him. (James 1:2–4, 12)

Humble yourselves, therefore, under God's
mighty hand, that he may lift you up in due time.
Cast all your anxiety on him because he cares for
you. (1 Peter 5:6–7)

Prayers

Lord, you are the reason for all my joy. Help
me to fix my eyes on you when my circumstances
are painful and hard.

Jesus, I choose to seek You in the midst of all my problems.

Guide me God to where you are calling me to witness to others.

Lord Jesus, we find hope and strength in knowing that Your light shines in the darkness, and the darkness has not overcome it. (David McCusland)

Jesus, show me your will for my life and help me obey in every area.

Inspirational Verses

Some people won't love you no matter what you do and some people won't stop loving you no matter what you do. Go where the love is. (The Book of Prosperity)

What do we do when there is a 'mountain' before us? We have two options: rely on our own strength or trust the Spirit's power. When we trust His power, He will either level the mountain or give us the strength and endurance to climb over it (Marvin Williams)

God sends vertical help by horizontal means. He sends us what we need through the help of others. (Marvin Williams)

Trust that an ending is always followed by a new beginning. (Author unknown)

When we honestly ask ourselves which person in our lives means the most to us, we often find that it is those who, instead of giving advice, solutions, or cures, have chosen rather to share our pain and touch our wounds with a warm and tender hand. (Henri Nouwen)

Two souls looked out at the world and saw the same thing. One was filled with joy, the other was filled with pain. It is not the thing we look upon that paints our point of view, but the heart through which we see it that gives our world its hue. (Dean Jackson)

You can't wait for everything to be perfect before you decide to enjoy your life. You will never have this day again, so make it count. (Unknown)

Sometimes you have to let go of the picture of what you thought it would be like and learn to find joy in the story you are actually living." (Rachel Marie Martin, *Finding Joy*)

Everyone you meet has a part to play in your story. And while some may take a chapter, others a paragraph, and most will be no more than scribbled notes in the margins. Someday you'll meet someone who will become so integral to your life you'll put their name in the title. (Beau Tiplin, *Life Stories*)

Sometimes being strong and moving on is the only choice you have. (Unknown)

Put on your Big Girl panties and deal with it. (Unknown)

Life is a whole, and good and ill must be accepted together. The journey has been enjoyable and well worth making-once. (Winston Churchill)

Courage is the first of all human qualities because it guarantees all others. (Winston Churchill)

To live in the religious spirit is not easy; the believer is continually on a deep sea 70,000 fathoms deep... It is a great thing floating on 70,000 fathoms of water and beyond all human aid to be happy; it is a little thing and not at all religious to swim in shallow water with a host of waders… No matter how long the religious man lies out there, it does not mean that little by little he will reach land again. He can become quiet, attain a sense of security that loves jest, and the merry mind. But to the last moment, he lives over 70,000 fathoms of water. ~ Soren Kierkegaard

In response to the "Why" questions many of us ask when we are faced with tragedy. "The first is that we shouldn't spend too much time trying to answer the 'why' questions: Why me? Why must people suffer? Why can't someone else get sick? We can't answer such things, and the questions themselves often are designed more to express our anguish than to solicit an answer. (From Tony's Snow's testimony)

The scars you share…become lighthouses for other people who are headed for the same rocks you hit. (Author unknown)

An Open Letter to Fred

F red,

    I call this an open letter because what I am writing to you, I want to openly share with others. During our marriage, we certainly had things we shared only with each other. I will take those treasured discussions with me when I die, never sharing with anyone else. Most of these things I shared with you while you were here on earth with me. Some I have shared with you in my thoughts since you have been gone.

    Honey, you truly are the best thing that ever happened to me. When we met, I was a twenty-two-year-old "kid" who had come out of a bad relationship that was toxic and would have destroyed me if I had stayed in it. I felt broken and defective and that I had let my family and God down.

    The first night we went out on our blind date, I was smitten with you. Between your laugh, your smile, your eyes, and your kindness, I couldn't help but start to fall for you. And what girl wouldn't have been swept off her feet by a firefighter who stopped for a chimney fire on the way to the movie? You asked me that night if you could kiss me good-night and I said "yes." When you kissed me, I literally tingled all over, I had never felt that way about anyone. When I told my mom about our date, I told her that you were the man for me and that I would marry you someday. I never thought we would have our first date on February 12, 1984, get engaged in June, and be married on October 20, 1984. There is no doubt in my mind that we would still be married if God had not called you home on September 22, 2016. It was a great ride, honey, just way too short.

    You were the perfect mate for me. While neither one of us was perfect, I truly believe we were perfect for each other. How you tolerated my idiosyncrasies amazes me: my quirkiness, my impatience, my need to travel, my ability to change my mind in a moment's notice, my snarky tone when tired, and the list goes on. You stood by me as I pursued my degrees and worked way too much at times. You kept me from taking myself too seriously, at least most of the time.

Of course, my ability to tolerate your ability to procrastinate and be the champion of passive-aggressive behavior was pretty awesome too! We were a pair, and what a pair we were. We supported each other through many trials and tribulations in our careers. When things were incredibly stressful and difficult in our jobs, we always had each other's back and gave each other support to get through the rough times.

You willingly came with me halfway around the world on a mission trip to Kenya. You came with Christopher and me on a mission trip to hot and humid North Carolina to repair roofs. You hiked Machu Picchu with me. You hiked down to the bottom of the Grand Canyon with me. You even sea kayaked with me, though you told me you would never do it again in no uncertain terms. I still smile when I see you in the back of the kayak while we paddled in the ocean and around the Bay of Fundy.

As much as you were the best travel partner ever, you were an even more amazing parenting partner. I cannot imagine raising sons with anyone but you. You were, and still are, the best role model our sons could have ever had. You showed them how to treat their mother with respect and love. You showed the boys how to treat women and how to be good husbands and fathers. Honey, you showed the boys the value of hard work and playing hard. You showed them what to take seriously and yet to not take themselves too seriously. You showed them a man can love, cry, and depend on a woman as well as to keep their faith in God.

As a life partner, you are unmatched. You were the hardest working, most devoted, and honest man I have ever known. As I try to take care of the household and the property, I simply do not know how you did it all. You worked, usually two to three jobs, you helped me raise the boys, you coached soccer and baseball, you helped me with Cub Scouts, you helped me garden/plant trees, the list goes on.

It makes me exhausted to think of all you did every day, and I apologize for days when I took you for granted. If I could say anything to you in person again other than "I love you," it would be to apologize if you ever felt I did not appreciate you.

Honey, someday I will be in heaven with you. I don't know what that will look like, and I don't know what we will look like. I don't understand what husbands and wives have as a relationship in heaven. I guess I will find that out some day. I can say that if it is better than what we had on earth, it will be truly amazing.

I want you to know how much we miss you here on earth with us. The boys are so much of you, and they give me such joy and strength. I look at them and some of the things they say and do, and they take my breath away. "Our girls" miss you and wish they had gotten more time with you. As much as I miss you, I am at peace knowing you are in a better place. You suffered with back and neck pain for years even before the brain cancer. To know you have no pain anymore gives me joy. I would never want you to ever suffer again. To know how much you missed your dad every day after his death, it makes me happy to know you are with him now. As much as you loved us and didn't want to go, I know how much you loved God. You are with your Heavenly Father as well as your earthly parents now. It must be spectacular in heaven!

Fred, you were my true love, and you always will be. Thank you for loving me even when I was acting unlovable. Thank you for showing me how to face death with grace and dignity. You were simply amazing. I hope you look down and smile and laugh at the dumb things I continue to do that made you laugh when you were here with me. There are times I can almost hear you say, "Kid, what are you doing?."

I will always love you and miss you, and I look forward to the day you are waiting for me as I cross through the thin veil.

All my love,
Karin

An Open Letter to My Sons

Nicolaus and Christopher, yes, I know to most people you are Nic and Chris, but to your dad and me, you will always be Nicolaus and Christopher. I want you to know that I would have never been able to get through the past two-plus years without your love and support. At times when I thought I simply could not go on, I looked at pictures of you, or talked to you on the phone, or texted, or saw you in person, and you gave me the strength to put one foot in front of the other.

I know your dad was not simply "Dad" to you. He was your coach, mentor, coworker, and best friend. I watched him beam with pride from the moment you were born until the day he became unresponsive. I believe part of the reason he lingered at the end was that he simply did not want to leave us—and especially you. He had such wonderful plans ahead of spending more time with you fishing, hiking, eating (as we know the man loved to eat), helping you with your future projects, and growing old while enjoying hanging out with you and your families.

Your dad lived each day to the fullest. He believed in "seizing the day," whether it was working all day, playing, or enjoying ice cream and a Snickers bar. He rarely missed the opportunity to enjoy being with family and friends and/or working. Since your dad has passed on, I have contemplated how much I miss his larger-than-life personality. I knew he lit up a room when he entered, but I truly did not appreciate it as much as I should have, but I see so much of his personality in both of you and it comforts me greatly.

Obviously, this was not your dad's plan, or mine, that he would leave us when he did. He told me for years he was going to "go kicking and screaming" because he had so much he wanted to do before he died. I will tell you though, he was at peace as he faced his death, and his deep faith gave him the strength he needed as the end drew near. I hope that despite maybe being mad at God or sometimes questioning your faith, you draw from your dad's strength and faith. It is the one thing that gave him the peace he needed—that he would be in heaven with all of us someday and into eternity.

I think your dad is proud of how you handled yourselves throughout his cancer path and since his death. You were attentive to him and me; you helped us however and whenever you were able; you have shown strength and weakness, which are incredibly masculine and human. You have honored him with how you talk about him and treat me.

You both are a mixture of your dad and me; I think you got the best parts of him, and I hope you have the same from me. You have his quick wit, determination, and soft heart surrounded by just a little crustiness. I think you got my "filter," even though the part of your dad in you challenges the filtering from me at times. His capacity to love was huge, and I see that in the two of you. Your dad did not have an easy life, and throughout his long firefighting career, there were difficult and dark times. He struggled occasionally with his job due to a variety of reasons, and there were periods of time he questioned if it was "right" for him. He knew, deep down, being a firefighter what he was meant to do, but honestly, the difficult times did make him question his career choice. I share this with you because I know there will be times you do the same, and I want you to know his struggles too. He would have shared this with you if he was here with you. Ultimately though, he always wanted for the two of you to do work that brought you a sense of joy and accomplishment. We joked as we were raising you that we hoped you would find careers that were "legal, ethical, and made you productive members of society." He was proud of your career choices, but really, he was proud of you both for the wonderful men you grew into; what you chose for careers was not as important.

I think I could write pages and pages on how much your dad loved you and how very proud he was to be your dad. I think he did a good job of showing you both how much he loved you. What he was most proud of was watching you become the men that you are and watching you as husbands, a father, an uncle, brothers, and sons, and having you honor your mom and dad. These are qualities that you modeled from him.

My heart breaks for you every day that you don't have him physically with you; however, when I look at you and watch you, I see him standing by you in spirit. I hope you feel his presence with you daily. It may not seem fair that your dad left us way too soon; on the other hand, he gave you more in your short lives than many children ever get from their dads in a much longer span of time. Your dad "showed up" for you every day, and many children cannot say that about their dad.

And finally, you are my pride and joy! Of the things I am most proud of, it is marrying your dad and raising the two of you with him. To say I have been blessed beyond measure by you is an understatement. Thank you for sharing a piece of your dad with me every time I see you or talk to you.

Love always,
Mom

An Open Letter to "My Girls"

Lisa and Michelle, I want to thank you openly for loving Dad and me. From the moment Nicolaus and Christopher introduced each of you to us, Dad and I felt you were the one for our son. We were so happy to welcome you into the family, and I could not be happier to have you as "my girls."

You didn't get to have Dad in your lives nearly long enough. I think you did get to see what a loving, big-hearted, hard-working man he was, and I am certain you can see much of him in Nicolaus and Christopher. You also get to "experience" how much of their dad they have in them when it comes to their sense of humor and "quirks." I will have to admit to contributing to some of their "quirkiness" as well, but I really feel they are so much their father in many, many ways.

I can tell you that Dad Schwan loved you both very much. He was always happy to see you and spend time with you. I want to really share openly with you how much your love and support has meant to me, particularly from the time Dad was diagnosed through the present time.

You both understood very quickly the enormity of the situation, and you stepped up to help me take care of Dad. I watched the sadness in your eyes when you visited, as you knew what was to come, and yet you put on your "game face" for us both to offer love and support and strength. Your love and support to your husbands through all of this was amazing. You understood that Dad was not just their father, but their best friend and mentor, and you realized how devastating the outcome was going to be for them.

I cannot begin to tell you how much I appreciate the fact that you allow me to laugh and cry and be my weird and quirky self

138

around you, and you continue to love me. Sometimes, daughters-in-law and mothers-in-law don't get along well; however, I feel so blessed that I have both of you who I love. I feel blessed that you freely share your love with me. You call me, text me, visit with me, and even travel with me. You have continued to support me throughout my Tar Pit path even though I know you are grieving as well.

I wish things would have been different, that Dad and I would have grown old together, and someday, you would have had discussions like "what are we going to do with Mom and Dad" or "what are they up to now" or "what trip are they taking next." I guess you will just have to have those conversations about me. I will try to not make a nuisance of myself, but my quirkiness may continue to be a challenge well into my old age.

To Jordyn and Eva, I wish very much that you would have had many, many more years with Papa Schwan. He loved you both very much and was so happy to be a grandfather—and especially of girls! We were so happy to become grandparents and could not have asked for two more sweet and adorable granddaughters. Please know that even though you can't see Papa Schwan anymore, he will always be in your heart and he is looking down from heaven and watching you grow up.

I look forward to many years of "Schwan women" activities. I was surrounded for years with testosterone, and it is nice to have some additional estrogen in the family. I am blessed and so very grateful to call you all "my girls."

Love always,
Mom (Grammie)

An Open Letter to My Parents and Siblings

"In-law" has not been a term that either Fred or I regularly used to talk about our families. He didn't think of my parents or my brother and his wife as in-laws nor did I consider his sisters and their spouses and his mother as in-laws. We did not consider Fred's mother's husband anyone other than dad. Having said all of that, Mom and Dad Wolf, Mom Rogers, Michael and Lori, Teresa and Jerry, Barb and Jim and Pat, this is for you.

Almost from the moment Fred and I started dating, we each were taken into our respective families. Mom and Dad Wolf, you loved Fred as your son, and Mom Schwan, you took me in as "her fourth daughter." Both of us felt so blessed to have our families love our chosen mate the way they did. When Dad Rogers entered our family, we loved him as "ours," and he loved us back.

I cannot begin to thank you all enough for the love and support you showed Fred and me during our entire marriage. You all took such an interest in us as a young couple and then as a couple with children and, finally, as a couple who had matured and grown into a long, successful married relationship together. So many memories—birthdays, holidays, family dinners, weddings, and simply life spent together in family times continue to bring me joy. We were blessed that both sides of the family took an interest in the other side, and you all considered every member as family, not just" Karin's" or" Fred's."

Mom Schwan Rogers, while I feel you are in heaven and cannot read the words as printed, I do know you can somehow see this message. Thank you from the bottom of my heart for sharing Fred so freely with me. Now, as a widow myself, I understand how much you depended on Fred after Dad Schwan died. You were never "needy" though. I understand how lonely you must have been after Dad Schwan's passing. Instead of complaining, you cheerfully handed Fred off to me, and you soldiered on. I knew you were incredibly strong, but I could not truly appreciate how much until after Fred died and I had to soldier on myself. I simply do not know how you kept your faith through the loss of two husbands and your beloved son, Fred. You were a class act all the way! I only wish I had been able to spend more time with you, learning how to be strong. You amaze me still.

Mom and Dad Wolf, thank you for your love and support. As a parent, I understand how difficult it is to see your child in pain and not be able to make everything better. It is a horrible feeling, one of feeling out of control and helpless. You have had to watch me grieve deeply, and you see the crushing pain I feel, and you know you cannot take that away. Thank you for being my rocks, for loving me when I am acting unlovable, for helping me care for Fred after his diagnosis, for mowing my lawn, for cooking for me, for simply being present with me when words will not work to explain the heartache. I am rich beyond measure with the love, patience, and support you have shown for me, and continue to show. Walking this path through the Tar Pit would have been exponentially more difficult without you there to shore me up. Thank you, thank you, thank you!

Michael and Lori, you stepped in seamlessly to help me get Fred to and from the James. You called to check on me, listening to me sob when I was trying to be strong during our phone conversations, stopped in to do "welfare checks" on me, and have loved and supported me through the really difficult and dark days. I feel so blessed to have you for my brother and sister. You continue to check on me and include me in your lives and I am grateful. Thank you for loving Fred as your brother; he loved you as his brother and sister. It was great fun to watch you all interact and play off of each other's sense of humor.

Barb, Jim, Pat, and Teresa, (and Jerry too), I cannot begin to express my gratitude for taking me in as your sister when Fred and

I got married. There hasn't been a day that I haven't felt part of the family. Your love and support through our marriage has been wonderful, but your continued love and support as "yours" is truly priceless. I have had the Schwan name now longer than I had Wolf as a last name. You continue to make me feel that I belong to you. Fred was so proud of all of you and loved you so much.

Barb, I could not have gotten through the days without your help. Your willingness to step in when Fred and I needed you is impressive. I know it was uncomfortable to become Fred's nurse so I could go to work, and yet, there you were, caring for him like you had done it for years. I know how overwhelmed I felt some days; I am sure it was overwhelming for you, and yet, there you were by my side.

Pat and Teresa, I know you prayed for us and did all you could. Your distance, Pat, and your own medical condition limited what you could do physically, but your spiritual strength and support meant just as much. Teresa, you have carried such a huge load for years as Jerry's caregiver, and my heart aches particularly for you, as I know how you feel to lose your husband and love of your life. You also lost your brother one month later. What a blow! Your strength and faith are inspirational.

I know that each of you continues to walk your own path through the Tar Pit. Yes, I lost Fred, but so did you. It does not go unnoticed that you all are grieving as well. I cannot ever really express my love and gratitude for all you have done for me and continue to do. The Tar Pit path is difficult, and yet it would be so much more so without you in my lives. I love you all and am forever grateful that God placed each of you into my life.

Mom, you are my rock! You were there from the moment I told you I thought Fred had a brain tumor prior to his diagnosis. You understood the gravity of the situation, and I did not have to explain. You could see it in my eyes, and you worked immediately to help me in every way you possibly could to ease my pain and help take care of Fred. You still watch me struggle and see through my facade when I am trying to be happy but am having a "sad day." Thank you for always being willing to lend a shoulder and let me "be" anyway I am feeling at that time and not trying to fix it. You understand completely the Tar Pit path.

Dad, thank you for just letting me "be" as well. You always have a cup of coffee waiting for me whenever I need to just sit and sip for a few minutes. I could not have taken care of the property the past three summers without your help in mowing. You have no idea the pressure you have taken off of me with all your help. I am grateful!

Michael Jon and Lori, you have been such sources of strength for me. Your assistance as regular "road warriors" during radiation treatments was priceless. Fred loved spending time with you, and I appreciated the help so very much. Your phone calls and visits during all of the time from Fred's diagnosis until now have been meaningful. I am grateful for both of you.

Words will never express my gratitude, but please know I am indeed grateful and love you all!

Karin

An Open Letter to Family, Friends, Coworkers, and the Community

Fred was definitely a family man; he was a true friend and believed in actively serving his community. While I understood what a community-focused man he was, I did not fully realize the impact he had on so many people in and around Ashland throughout his entire life until he was diagnosed.

To those who have shared your remembrances of Fred, thank you. Your stories have given me such joy even through my tears. The consistent theme I have heard from all of you is that Fred was kind, never a bully, always took the side of the underdog, and was incredibly tenacious. School classmates have shared that he was never a trouble maker though, yes, a little ornery. Fire department colleagues have told me wonderfully moving and funny stories of Fred at work and at play. He had told me some of them, but to hear them from another perspective and new stories I hadn't yet heard meant so much.

The outpouring of love and support we received almost from the moment of Fred's diagnosis was remarkable. You have no idea how much your cards, letters, texts, Facebook messages, calls, and visits meant to us, particularly to Fred. He was truly overwhelmed and deeply moved. Your love and support helped to sustain him to the end. I think part of the reason it took so long in the final days is that he really loved so many people and didn't want to leave us quite yet, even though he knew heaven was going to be wonderful.

I could not have continued to work and take care of Fred if it were not for the support I received from you. The assistance with trips to and from the James for radiation treatments, the time spent with Fred so I could go to work, the shoulder to cry on so Fred did not see me break down crying at home—all of this and more was priceless.

To our aunts, uncles, cousins, nieces, and nephews, you have no idea the impact you had on us. From the moment Fred was diagnosed, your pouring of love and support helped to lift us up. The visits seemed to be heaven-sent as they came at times when I was so scared and needed someone to lean on so I could be strong for Fred. The phone calls to check on us, the meals you brought, the texts just to say "hi," the trips back from Colorado, meeting us in Columbus for radiation treatments/surgery, and family meals, and the list goes on, were all appreciated more than you will ever know. You all have continued to buoy up me, Nicolaus, Lisa, Christopher, and Michelle, and I am so grateful for all of you.

To all who have impacted our lives through the Tar Pit path, I have not listed each and every one of you as I am sure I would miss someone, and the last thing I want to do is leave someone out. You have made a lasting impact. Please know that your cards, prayers, texts, Facebook messages, as well as your hugs and shoulders to lean on have made all the difference in the world to me. You all help to stabilize me and keep me trudging forward through the Tar Pit.

Love,
Karin

Facebook Posts 2016

*M*_{*ay 9*}

To all our FB friends and family, thank you for your prayers and kind thoughts. It can't be stressed enough how much that means. To all my nurse friends, Happy Nurses' Day, you have no idea how a smile, a tender touch and gentle voice means from this side of things. It has been a whirlwind couple of days and to say this is overwhelming is an understatement. To Tabi Alexander, your sweet smile today made your uncle and me feel so much better. To our wonderful sons and daughters in law, Nic Schwan, Chris Schwan, Lisa Schwan and Michelle Schwan, we could not have the strength to get through this without you. Fred Wolf, Kay Wolf, Michael Wolf, Lori Savick Wolf, Jared Wolf, Joshua Wolf, Lynzie Chandler, thank you for the calls, text, support and prayers. Fred's sisters, Barb, Pat, and Teresa, have been so sweet and caring. To those I haven't mentioned by name, you are in our hearts and are grateful for your support. Please pray for strength for us, wisdom for those caring for Fred, and the best outcome possible. God has His plan and while I may not understand it, I know that all things work for His glory.

May 10

I apologize for the drama, not really how we want to communicate with you all but I guess this the best way to do so. Just got an update from the Surgery Hostess and Fred's surgery started at 0838 today. Pray please for healing hands in the OR and that Fred comes through this first surgery in great shape. We will not know definitive results until next week and then the really tough stuff begins. I will send out updates as I am able. I am overwhelmed and humbled by your prayers and support. Thanks!!

May 11

OK FB friends and family. I thought I would get an update out on Fred. It is a glioblastoma brain tumor. Don't look it up as they are not all the same and they are doing DNA testing on the biopsy specimens to see the best way to treat it. It is not curable but hopefully can be treated to improve quality of life. Chemo, radiation, both, we do not yet know, and I do not know if surgery is an option. Funny that this girl, who is such a control freak, can do nothing to control any of this. God has a way of leading us on a path we do not expect. Fred specifically told me it was OK to share, so I am following his wishes. We have had some pretty serious discussions today and we know it is going to be hard and rocky. We also know we have a truly wonderful team of family and friends and you have no idea how much that means to both of us as well as Nicolaus, Christopher, Lisa, and Michelle, and our parents, siblings, nephews, nieces, and our special Miss J and Baby Schwan on the way. I do want to make sure people understand that we chose OSU for a variety of reasons. One, niece Tabi Alexander works here and having a smiling face of a loved family member each day to check on us has meant so much. Having Sue Wilder close in case I need a nurse friend or place to go helps too. We have had amazing care. Gotta go.

May 13

A quick update. We are home. It has been a big day of adjusting to our new normal. A big thanks to Nic Schwan and Lisa Schwan for making the house "Fred Friendly." My hope is to be on some form of reasonable schedule so those wanting to visit or spend part of a day while I work will be welcome. Once we know when radiation therapy starts anyone wishing to transport a day for the M-F treatments please let me know. It will be a trip to The James but the treatment is actually pretty short, more details to come. We are humbled by everyone's prayers and good wishes. You are amazing.

May 15

Today I decided I needed positivity in my life so I am starting on my "attitude of gratitude." I am grateful that I don't have 8–10 flats of flowers and vegetables to be planted like I normally do as we have frost warnings in the area. I am grateful I don't have plants that I have to cover tonight in the cold. Normally I am working on my gardens and flower pots at this time of Spring but we have been preoccupied. I am grateful for the man sleeping beside me and treasure even his snoring tonight. Sleep well.

May 19

I am posting with Fred's permission. Thank you to all who have been keeping us in your thoughts and prayers. Thank you as well for the hugs, cards, and yes, even tears. Your support is amazing. Many have asked if we saw the Duke University information on the breakthrough treatment they are doing in the field of glioblastoma treatment. In fact, I overnight Fed ex shipped the MRI CD to Duke Tuesday after registering on-line Sunday night after watching *60 Minutes*. We received a call Tuesday morning from Duke with instructions on where to ship the CD. The CD arrived yesterday morning and last night, about 9:30 pm we received a call from one of the physicians at Duke doing the research, Dr. Friedman. Impressive turn-around. He said that there is nothing Duke can offer that we can't get at The James. It was good news/bad news. No additional travel, but no chance at a "miracle cure" at Duke. Dr. Friedman did give me the name of an additional drug he suggests we use for treatment as adjunctive treatment to the oral chemo and radiation. So, prayer warriors, please keep the prayers coming for healing. We do believe with God all things are possible. The outcome will be God's plan. We head back to the The James next week for the treatment plan and getting radiation treatments set up. If you have my phone number and can help with transport, please text me. You can also message me. Prayers, driving, good wishes, etc. are all wonderful and we so appreciate all of you.

May 23

An update: we spent a very long day at The James today at OSU Medical Center. The entire team there is amazing and we are grateful for their dedication. The tumor is indeed a glioblastoma multiforme, not the kind of brain tumor to have, nor in a good location. We really already knew that part, but it was confirmed. The kernel of good news is that the DNA testing on the tumor showed it to be more susceptible to chemo and radiation than most glioblastomas and it does make Fred eligible for a clinical trial also. As clinical trials go though, when they are set up double-blinded placebo, you may or may not get the actual drug. We know though that clinical trials can help the person in the trial but mostly they help those coming after. Fred's dad was in a clinical trial and who knows how many he may have helped in his battle with cancer. (Come to find out it was a hemangioblastoma not a glio.) At any rate, we start the chemo-radiation treatments next week. There will be 30 treatments, 5 days per week. We are so grateful for your prayers; they really do hold us up. We also thank those who have provided us with gas and food gift cards. They will certainly come in handy! I am getting directions written up and instructions for what to do when getting to The James. It is easy to get to, then valet park, then up the elevator to second floor for a 15-minute treatment (but probably an hour wait in total), back to the valet pick up and head home. If anyone would like to drive an afternoon please let me know. It's not something I expect but am grateful for anyone wanting to help and I will have a gas card to offset your expenses. We cannot express what your kindness and support mean to our family; we are humbled. I want to share the Psalm verse for the day Fred had the biopsy, May 10 and then for today, May 23. "Many are the afflictions of the righteous: but The Lord delivereth him out of them all" (May 10). "In the day of my trouble I will call upon Thee: for Thou wilt answer me." (May 23). God is good and we are blessed.

May 25

Happiness is…letting go of what you think your Life is supposed to look like…

And celebrating it for everything that it is…"

Author: Mandy Hale

June 2

An attitude of gratitude. Today we began the radiation and last night the chemotherapy, as we fight what I call "the dragon" (aka Fred's tumor). Our prayers are that God uses the chemo and radiation as the vehicle for His power to heal Fred. We do not know what is before us, but we do know that we are grateful for our time together. We feel blessed for the outpouring of love and support from friends and family. We have been overwhelmed by so many who have donated: their time as well as buying and planting flowers and vegetables, gifts cards for fuel and food for those making the trips with Fred up and down 71 for treatments, meals delivered to our home, auctioning of a bedliner for cash, offers to clean the house, mow the lawn, and anything else we needed. Really though, the most important in all of this is everyone's love and prayers. You are an amazing group of people. We are trying to personally thank you all, if we miss someone please forgive us. You are our rocks!

June 8

An update: it has been an up and down week. We had a wonderful weekend with friends and family. Thanks to Liz Leasure for arranging a family photo with Mauer Photography and a big thanks to John Mauer for donating his time and talent. We are touched! Our venue was the Rose Garden at Trinity Lutheran Church. This is the church where we were married, the boys were baptized and confirmed, and Nicolaus and Lisa were married, and where we attend church. John is a terrific photographer and even though I don't like getting my picture taken, this was such a special time for Fred, the boys and their wives, and Miss J. We then had a family meal together at our house and a visit from Josh Wolf and Caroline Sutherland. The great weekend was followed by crushing news on Monday. Fred will not be able to be in the clinical trial since not enough tumor tissue was left from testing at The James to send to the clinical trial clearinghouse. That was bad enough but then Fred's lab work was very abnormal and we were told that if his labs didn't improve today, they would stop the chemo and continue only the radiation. Many tears and prayers later and medication adjustments and today the labs are still elevated but were improved so we will continue chemo with the radiation for now. Thank you to all who send good wishes, keep praying for strength and healing, who offered to drive to/from The James, and have donated gas/food cards. We are quite frankly overwhelmed by everyone's love and support. You amaze us. Please keep up with prayers for healing and strength as we continue walk the path God puts before us. This is tough stuff but we know we are blessed.

July 19

I didn't get pictures of all our "Road Warriors" and I apologize. Ken Rosser, Matt Chandler, Bob and Nancy Davis, and Nancy Smith I somehow missed. If I started to list everyone who has sent cards, gift cards, prayers, made meals, mowed the lawn, etc. I know I would miss someone and the list would be huge. Please know, you all continue to be our rocks through this process. Chemo and radiation are done and we now are in a wait and see pattern until the repeat MRI in early August and then a follow up at The James. Fred's platelets are still dropping so we pray that turns around soon, but otherwise he looks great, is doing so much better, and continues to keep a positive attitude and inspires me daily. I know I would not handle myself with the grace that he has shown. I apparently knew what I was doing when I said "yes" 32 years ago. A special thanks to John Mauer for taking truly beautiful family photos for us and I wish I could post them but since they are professionally copywritten I won't without John's permission. We are so touched by his and his staff's generosity. My mom, Kay Wolf, and sister Barb Chandler have been such a tremendous support as "the nannies" so I can continue to work. I simply could not make it without them. As we await the very special delivery of our first grandbaby (Christopher and Michelle's child), we are grateful to be able to experience this together. We were equally blessed to share a special day with Nicolaus and Lisa, as Nicolaus was sworn into Ashland Fire Department. We have had gifts cards from members of the Ashland HS Class of 1971 and Hillsdale Class of 1979, Ashland, Mifflin, and Hayesville Fire Departments, and many friends from across the area and country. The love and support I feel every day from my co-workers at UH-Samaritan has pulled me through when I am feeling my lowest. We had a healing service at Mohicanville United Church as a gift from my friend Krystal Raubenolt who offered it. I spoke at the youth group there last year about the Ethiopia Medical Mission Trip and the youth, pastor, Krystal, and Max and Karla Fulk gave us such a gift back with a healing service. Trinity Lutheran Church has been so supportive and wraps us in love every week when we worship. Many other churches send weekly get well and inspirational cards. We just can't say enough how grateful we are and how blessed we feel from the community of family and friends far and near. We do not know where the future takes us and what it holds for us but we are thankful that so many of you and many others have been with us along the way. It is a crazy and out of control world and yet we feel so grounded by all the love and support.

August 9

As promised, here is the update from today's visit to The James with Fred. As we expected, the tumor has grown a little, and there is still swelling from radiation so his symptoms are a result of those two things. An increase in steroids has helped to decrease symptoms although they have not completely resolved. While we were initially told the tumor was large and too deep to be able to be surgically removed, there is now discussion that surgery and 1 of 2 other additional chemo/immunotherapy agents in clinical trials may be options. Fred's case will be discussed at The Tumor Board on Thursday and we will get a call letting us know if the surgeon wants to meet with us again. If the trials aren't available then we will do more chemo or look at other clinical trials available at other research centers. Glioblastomas are very aggressive but there is a great deal of research going on right now and we pray that a breakthrough comes through any day. We have so much to be grateful for and try to focus on that every day. It was good to have Nicolaus with us today. Ice cream at Ollie's in Delaware on the way home certainly was comfort food! So grateful for our family and friends and all the love and support and prayers. God is good and He will continue to hold us in His arms.

August 11

So, another change in plans. We will see the surgeon next week to discuss another clinical trial, different than the 2 we discussed Tuesday. Clinical trials and oncology are moving targets.

This trial is not a double blinded placebo trial which means if Fred qualifies for the repeat brain biopsy and the trial he will receive additional treatment targeted for the DNA match of the drug to the tumor. We pray God guides us in the best decision possible.

All this is going on as we wait for the imminent birth of our first grand baby. We have our beautiful granddaughter Jordyn who came into our lives when she was 2 but this is the first grand baby, exciting stuff.

It truly is a miracle of life as we all face so much pain and sadness in the world. Faith and hope are those things we must never lose sight of, for those are the things that keep us going. Please keep your prayers going for healing for all who fight the cancer battle.

August 18

To me, grief is like a Tar Pit, we can't go around it, over it or avoid it, we must go through if we are to somehow have resolution of our grief. Some don't ever make it through the pit and some trudge along, some go through it alone, and some have company along the way.

September 16

The last 2 days have been a whirlwind. We have been blessed by many visits from family and friends and even had our lawn mowed and trimmed by amazing friends. Fred is growing weaker and sleeps most of the time due to an overwhelming feeling of fatigue, though not seemingly painful which is a blessing. We know the end is coming near and he teaches me daily how to face death with grace and dignity. So many have given us comfort and that is what God desires. We know that life on earth is but a snapshot of eternity. Thank you for your loving support and prayers as that helps to sustain us

September 18

An update: while Fred is still not having pain, it was a very restless night. This AM we talked and felt Hospice would help with symptom control. We were blessed with a wonderful visit by Chris Schmidt and Chad Buzzard. What great friends! God is amazing that He continues to give us support through family and friends.

September 20

As I sit during my shift for Fred's bedside vigil, it is both agonizing and peaceful in an odd sort of way. I truly think the spirit is willing to go, but the body still struggles to stay. (Funny that I frequently "gently pushed," OK, nagged, Fred about eating healthier and now because he was in relatively good health the struggle is taking longer). So many times, I sat with families as they too kept the bedside vigil. What is evident to me today is that it is in the "showing up" or presence that we as humans give the gift of ourselves to each other. That may not mean actually being present physically for that person, but simply giving of oneself. So many people have shown up for us through cards, calls, emails, or FB replies and posts. We have had meals delivered, meals and services offered if we needed them, the lawn mowed, vegetables and flowers planted, hugs as I pass through the hall at work or when sitting at my desk just trying to put one thought together to get through the day. The love and compassion you have shown Fred, me, "the boys" and their wives, our parents and siblings, and the rest of our family has been comforting and humbling. I imagine as the next few days pass, we will have many more people "show up" in our lives. That's one thing that struck me about Fred from the very early days together, he showed up for his family, his friends, his beloved fire department brothers, and his community. Every day of our sons lives he "showed up," even if he was on duty and couldn't be physically present, our sons and I always knew he was thinking of us. This is the very real and raw part of the human condition now, and you all have shown up for us. Thank you, "for the greatest of these is love."

September 21

Keeping a bedside vigil as someone passes from this world to eternity is hard to watch but I am taken aback by the hard work that person must go through to leave. Although I have been with many dying patients in my career, this certainly is the most difficult yet. While each day we live, we are one day closer to death, it is in watching the dying that I think we actually understand living. As we make connections with others, build relationships, and "show up" for our family and friends, it is like a tightly woven web of gold, precious and fine. We hold fast to that web during life and that sustains us when we hit the difficult times. It makes sense that as we die, we must detach from each thread to move on. Today, there have been many friends who have stopped to say goodbye to Fred, all of you who stopped, emailed, texted, called, messaged, posted on FB, you are the threads and I now understand why this is taking so long for him to go. He faced this head on, told me he was not scared to die, and knew that he was going to be in eternity with God. But first, he has to detach, thread by thread, and for a man who has been so beloved, that's a lot of threads! So, while it seems agonizing to all of us watching and keeping the vigil, I hope you all feel his good-bye. You continue to sustain us daily!

September 22

Our vigil continues... He must have more threads to unbind from his web of life. As I try to be strong and keep putting one foot in front of the other, I try to think of those pearls people have given me to help me get through difficult times. When Christopher deployed to Afghanistan I thought my heart would break, I was so overwhelmed with worry and fear about what might happen. It was very hard for me to function. A physician colleague, Dr. Jim Mooney, asked me, "Karin, do you believe Christopher is a gift from God and is God's child too"? I answered, "of course"!! He said "then realize, he never really was all yours, he is God's too, and in due time God calls His children home." I have thought a great deal about that through the night. When my brother and I, Michael Wolf, were growing up in Jeromesville, we spent summers riding our bikes, playing ball at the park and going to play at friends' houses. Mom and Dad willingly let us go but they also knew we would be home when called or at the appointed time. I think this life is like that, we get to come to "play" for a while because God knows we will come home to Him at the appointed time. This does comfort me knowing he is going home soon. And knowing Fred, he will want pizza, ice cream, and cookies waiting for him when he gets there.

September 22

Today ended a beautiful chapter in my book of life. It was long, but not long enough, and full of adventure, a little drama and a whole lot of love. Just like a great book, you know it will end but you don't want it to. You can re-read the book but it always ends the same. Fred and I started our grieving process at his diagnosis as we both knew how it was going to end. Instead of feeling sorry for himself or becoming bitter and pushing us away, Fred embraced us even more and his motto became "seize the day." As I have said before, Fred never ceased to amaze me and I have been humbled by his strength and attitude. It was a difficult few days for all of us, particularly Fred. The dying process is hard work but it does make me value the sanctity of life even more. Thank you from the bottom of my heart to all who have supported us through the cancer path. I refuse to call it a journey. (To me, journeys should be something I choose to go on and involve plane tickets), but it has been a path we all walked together. My heart has a hole that will never fill, but my faith in God and belief that one day we will all be together with God does sustain me.

September 24

As so many of us grieve now and ask the "why did this happen question," remember we are human and we cannot comprehend God's thoughts. Asking why does not change the outcome and it wastes precious energy we can put toward "showing up" for others in our lives. Let us not be bitter, angry, or question God. Let us walk through the tar pit of grief, arm in arm with our gaze fixed on the other side where we will create the new normal without Fred with us physically, but always with us in spirit. He would be honored.

September 25

I had to smile as I got my "sign from Heaven just now." As you can imagine, I am emotional and my typical scattered activity is even worse. Before Fred became unresponsive, I asked him to send me a sign, if he could, that he made it to Heaven and was now happy and at peace. I walked into what we transformed into "the day room," aka Nicolaus' old bedroom for some strange reason today. I looked in the corner of the closet where there are still some old photo albums. I pulled one out and it was filled with pictures from a family trip out West in 1995. In that album was a post card Fred had written to his crew at Ashland Fire Department telling of our trip and the still visible scars in Yellowstone from the fires of 1988. There is also a picture of Fred with the Combat Challenge winner at the Casper, WY Fire station. Fred was so proud of being able to compete and do well in the "old guys" category of the Firefighter Combat Challenge. This trip was the one where we came upon a canyon fire in the wilderness. Fred emptied our cooler and ran down the ravine to the river to begin putting out the fire. I took the boys and drove to the nearest town to alert the volunteer FD. Fred was still hauling water to the fire when the trucks and volunteers arrived. While I cried as I looked at the pictures and his beautiful handwriting on the post card (his handwriting had gotten illegible from the effects of the tumor), I smiled as I knew I had my sign. Fred is safely in the arms of God, enjoying time with his beloved Dad and many friends and family who welcomed him home with open arms. My heart is breaking but I know my man finally made it home.

October 20

32 years ago, October 20th, 1984, I married the love of my life. I certainly wasn't expecting things to end the way they did. Hard to believe it has been 4 weeks since Fred died. It seems like yesterday and yet it seems like forever ago when I held his hand and kissed him. I am blessed to have had this wonderful man in my life and so grateful that we had 2 amazing sons who have now given us 2 daughters and 2 granddaughters. This is the first of many "firsts" throughout this year without Fred and the sadness is overwhelming at times. I am grateful for family and friends who patiently watch me try to hold in the tears, give me a hug, or tell me they are thinking of me and the rest of the family. Every day I know that God sustains me and I can lean on Him to carry me through the darkest of times and

WALKING THE TAR PIT

lead me through the "Tar Pit" of grief. Happy Anniversary Fred Schwan, I sure do miss you!

November 3

This week has been a roller coaster of emotions finally another step forward in the Tar Pit of grief. After coming home from a mini-vacation this past weekend, it hit me that Fred is gone. Not that I didn't realize it before but when a loved one dies, particularly a spouse, there is so much to do just to keep the household running, that for weeks I was on autopilot. Arriving home to an empty and quiet house in the wee hours of Sunday morning was tough but Sunday brought unpacking and laundry activities so I did well, or so I thought. On Monday and Tuesday however I was neck deep in The Tar Pit. I have been faithful with my devotions which keep me trying to step forward. I was blessed with cards and supportive notes in them at just the right time this week as well. The devotional yesterday was a breakthrough and I wanted to share for all in The Tar Pit too. It comes from the book "Healing After Loss" by Martha Whitmore Hickman. "Living on memories, clinging to relics and photographs, is an illusion. Like the food offered one in dreams, it will not nourish; no growth or rebirth will come from it… Anne Morrow Lindbergh." It goes on to say that…" shrines have their place, but they are poor backgrounds for life in the present moment." And so it goes, while I miss Fred so deeply that it hurts, no amount of daily sadness will bring him back. I have been given "the present" and that is a gift. I can choose to be thankful for my gift, the present, and savor the past with Fred but I cannot change the facts or circumstances that surround me; he is gone from this world and passed through the thin veil to Heaven. I never noticed Paul's references to "the veil" until this week as I am reading through Hebrews. This week is "All Saints" weekend at church and all who have gone through the thin veil before us this year will be celebrated. They are with our Heavenly Father and experiencing amazing peace. While I know I will cry as Fred's name is read, I will also be joyful in knowing he is experiencing peace and joy and will be waiting for me some day as I cross through the thin veil to Heaven. I still have a long walk through The Tar Pit ahead but am so grateful for those who come along side of me and help me to keep going. To you who have emailed, called, sent cards, prayed for me or stopped by my office to just "check in," THANK YOU! I will focus on the task at hand, walking through The Tar Pit of grief.

November 17

"It's the great mystery of human life that old grief passes gradually into quiet tender joy"
—Fyodor Dostoevsky

May your weekend be full of tender joy

November 18

Every day I am humbled by so many people who touch my life with prayers, words of encouragement, a hug, a card, etc. I see people who have gone before me through The Tar Pit and they inspire me to keep going and be grateful for all that I had with Fred and still have. God has a way of putting people in our lives at the perfect time. So even though the tears still come way too often and easily, I am truly grateful for so much: faith, family, friends. We really don't need more than that as we face what is before us each day.

December 23

Today several people asked if I had a tree decorated and if I was celebrating Christmas because of Fred's recent death. Comments like "You probably don't feel like celebrating Christmas" are certainly ways to acknowledge grief however I want to share that the "real "meaning of Christmas is Christ and His birth. It is when we are in our deepest and darkest part of The Tar Pit of grief that the light of the Christ child is the only thing that makes us continue to move forward. Ultimately His death and resurrection is what gives us the assured hope of being with our loved ones who have passed through the thin veil. It has been easy for me to "check out" from all that isn't really Christmas and yet focus on the true meaning. I would gladly have more days with Fred on earth but instead I know I will have eternity with him and God in heaven. For those grieving, look toward the light of the Christ child and may you keep moving ahead to the other side of The Tar Pit. Merry Christmas!

Facebook Posts 2017

J *anuary 22*

As I continue through the Tar Pit, some days give me more clarity than others. And some days, when I am feeling sorry for myself, tired, or get too self-absorbed, it is easy to take steps backward. I really want to keep moving forward. I believe there will be something good, and positive, and bright once I get through the pit. I wonder how long it will take and that's the impatient person in me that "wants to know" and "to have a schedule." Fred and I talked almost every day about "what's the plan for the day" since our schedules were so filled, sometimes with trivial stuff it seems now.

God does have plans for us, He just asks us to trust Him. It is in our humanness that we fight "the plan" and try to have our own way. That rarely goes well in the long run.

My devotional today spoke of our seeking "the why" when things don't go our way. We question why we didn't get the job we wanted, why we couldn't have children, why we suffer, and yes, why we have had the loss of a loved one. We tend to think: "why did God let this happen if He loved us," "Maybe there isn't a God," and the list goes on.

Here was my answer in my devotional from Our Daily Bread: "Does God care? His Son's death on our behalf, which will ultimately destroy all pain, sorrow, suffering, and death for eternity, answers that question. For God, who said 'Let light shine out of darkness', made His light shine in our hearts to give us the light of the knowledge of God's glory displayed in the face of Christ."

When I think of the face of Christ, dying on the cross for our salvation, and the pain He suffered, and the sacrifice of Christ and God, His Father, it really does bring me back to the reality that while our loss of Fred was a huge loss, it was Fred's gain to Christ, and we have that same opportunity someday. It doesn't mean I don't still grieve and miss Fred's smile, his big bear-paw hugs, his sense of humor, and yes, his hats sitting on my kitchen table which drove me crazy. It does mean that I think I have the "why" question answered. Sin entered the world through the fall of Adam and Eve, God fixed it through Christ's death, and we all reap the ultimate benefit when we die. So "the plan" really was laid out for me, for us, thousands of years ago. Hum…, makes my need to "have a plan" incredibly trivial.

May we all keep moving forward through our tar pits, there is a plan for us as we get through it.

January 29

Missing my man today. Maybe it is because the snow and icy roads make me think of him out salting and plowing for many years in the wee hours of the day and late into the night. Sometimes sleeping in his truck for a few hours so he could keep plowing for sometimes days on end. All my years of whining about the salt on my kitchen floor from his Carhart bibs really seems incredibly shallow now. So… I was feeling sorry for myself as I went out to walk the dog, take care of the cats, feed the birds, etc. I walked out to get the Sunday newspaper and saw 2 hearts in the snow at the end of the drive. I know it is from the newspaper deliverer backing into the drive and pulling out but it really was like it was a gift from Fred telling me he loves me and misses me too. To all, I hope your day is filled with love.

February 18

Notes from The Tar Pit: Several steps forward this week, particularly today. Fred and I enjoyed working outside on projects, whether it be picking up sticks, raking the old leaves off of fresh growth in the Spring, or getting the garden ready to plant. Our time was so precious together because of our professions, which kept us away from each other more often than they should. This past Fall, I did what had to be done to get the property winterized but I admit it was with such a heavy heart and MANY tears and tissues. It truly was out of necessity, not any joy. That's the thing about grief, we often "get through" activities but it is with sadness and heaviness, and with great difficulty. The world seems in slow motion but spinning out of control at the same time. Today was different. I did my morning "chores" of walking the dog, taking care of the cats, feeding the birds, etc. with a feeling of enjoyment in the moment. That has been many months in coming. Fred and I used to say "So this is what it is like to spend time together" as we worked outside. We laughed and talked of how "when we both retire" we will have so much fun being together. Sadly, that was not how it worked, however what great times we had regardless of the shortened timeframe. I admit, as I took a rest from raking leaves and picking up sticks early this AM and watched the birds in the backyard, I did shed a few tears. It wasn't the uncontrollable sobbing that would have come upon me months, or even weeks ago. I am sure there will be something that comes along and I will take a backward step in The Tar Pit. For those of you ahead of me, thanks for showing me the way. Almost everyday someone touches me in ways they do not know to inspire me to keep moving. For those of you walking hand in hand with me, hold on, we will get through it. God is right there with us. For those of you just stepping into The Tar Pit, please know it does get more "tolerable" and manageable; it is hard to use the word "better" yet.

March 5

In the Fall of 2006, Pastor Mitchell from Trinity Lutheran Church called us and asked if we would be interested in going on a mission trip. It would be to Kenya with another couple from Trinity, in February 2007. At first, we thought he was kidding and we told him we would need to think about it. Time was short however as we would need to begin the process of renewing our passports and getting the immunizations required for a trip to a developing country in Africa. Initially Fred said "no," but after prayer he changed his mind as he knew how much I wanted to go. This began our passion for mission work, and renewed our strong interest in international travel.

While there, we ministered to some of the poorest people in Kenya and in Africa. We were so inspired that the poor living in the slums of Nairobi had such a love for God and Jesus as their Savior. Despite all they lacked materially, they certain had plenty in their faith.

Fred, Christopher, and I went on another mission trip in the summer of 2008 to North Carolina with Trinity. While some we served were very poor, most were living in better conditions than those in the slums of Nairobi. And yet, there were those living in conditions as dire, yes, here in the USA! Several years later I was honored to go to Joplin, MO, the year after the devastating tornadoes with the youth of Trinity again.

While Fred was not able to go in body with our group to Ethiopia, he was there in spirit. The timing of the trip always coincided with snow plow season and it was difficult for him to be gone. He never "openly" complained about all the supplies that accumulated all year long and the multiple suitcases laying around the living room for weeks before the trip as we packed supplies. He drove our group to and from the airport each time, and prayed for our safety while we were gone.

When we completed the mission trip in Nairobi, we went on a safari to the Masai Mara. We found a print of the giraffes and elephants on the Masai Mara and always planned to get it in a frame and hung on the wall in the house. Today, I finally got it hung. It is bright and beautiful and reminds me that despite all the darkness in the world there is hope in Jesus Christ as The True Light of the World.

I hope this inspires you this Lenten season to listen to the still small voice inside of you, that of God guiding you in the ways you should go. I never imagined a call back in 2006 would have led Fred and I to the places we went and experiences we had.

I also ask for your support of the 3rd Annual Missions Auction at Trinity Lutheran Church, Ashland, OH on March 24th and 25th. Proceeds benefit the Ethiopia Medical Missions Trip and the Youth Mission Project. There is a dinner on the 24th with a preview of the auction items and the auction begins Saturday morning with a silent auction and bake sale as well. If you can't attend, please pray for a successful auction.

April 2

Update from the Tar Pit: This year Lent has been a particularly meaningful time for me. This period of the year is the time I try to come back to "my center" and contemplate the true meaning of what it is I am supposed to be doing as a Christian. I must admit though, it usually isn't super successful and I get distracted by work, "getting ready for Spring," planning the next big adventure, etc. I usually get to Easter rather disappointed in my inability to focus for a mere 6 weeks when I know I have been blessed with so much. This year, due to circumstances way beyond my control, I have spent more time in slowing down in the journey through Lent.

It is easy to feel sorry for ourselves when we lose great loves in our lives, or watch someone we love suffer as they near death. Honestly, it is the hardest thing I have ever done, and as our family watches it coming again, the wounds open and bleed a little more. And yet, it points to the reality that life here on earth is really less that a blink in time of eternity. Any suffering or pain is less than a bee sting in depth and length of time, and will soon be gone. Eternity with God with be free of pain and suffering. It's hard to keep that in focus though when walking through the thick, sticky, sometimes suffocating Tar Pit.

I've had interesting conversations with people who struggle to know "the why" of someone young dying or why the suffering occurs as we near death. We humans are so funny because we think if we just knew "the why" we would understand it all.

For those who are parents, or have been around children, or remember when you were a child, which is pretty much everyone, we remember when children ask "the why" to the point of frustration of everyone's part. Sometimes the answer is easy "you have to wear a coat because it is snowing out" or "you have to hold my hand because we are crossing the street." Sometimes the answers aren't as easily expressed and the answer is "Because I told you so" or "Because I am your Mom/Dad." In the end, the parent or adult with the child's best interest prevails and life goes on. I suppose it is that same way with God our Father. We want to know "the why" and sometimes it is obvious. Sometimes we listen and often we do not, so He must intercede on our behalf and say "Because,"

I used to ask the "why's" to God all the time and I am sure He wondered when I would stop to listen. This Lenten season I think I have listened a little more and actually asked "the why" must less often. As humans we just can't comprehend "the why." I realize though that feeling blessed for the time we do have with our loved ones is a way of thanking God for giving them to us for a little while on this earth. The time we get may not be meeting our timeline but it does meet God's.

As Easter nears it means so much more this year to know that someday we get to be joined with our loved ones in eternity. I suppose I will get all my questions of "why" answered at that time or maybe it won't really matter anymore.

April 10

Our amazing Mom (Schwan)Rogers went to be with her Lord today. She was such a wonderful woman and I am forever grateful at how she welcomed me into the family from the first time I met her. She had lost the love of her life, Fred's dad, only a short time prior to Fred and I meeting. In her grief she freely shared Fred with me and I know it had to be difficult. I smile when I think of her in Heaven with her "Freds" and Dad Rogers, as well as her parents and many siblings. While we grieve her leaving us what a glorious day in Heaven.

April 10

My last FB post for the night. Having spent a great deal of time at the bedside of dying loved ones over the past months I have had opportunity to reflect deeply on life, death and faith. I think the difference between having faith in God, life everlasting, Jesus and redemption is that as you watch a loved one die with faith, you feel sad but at the same time you feel joy for knowing where your loved one is going. When we have no faith, we only feel sadness and pain. Faith allows us to look past ourselves toward "the great beyond." Having no faith makes us only focus on self and our loss. This is such a bittersweet time and yet, Holy Week is the perfect time to grieve and yet celebrate. God certainly has good timing.

April 17

What a difference a year makes. One year ago, Fred and I were on a trip of a lifetime. We always wanted to go to Australia and New Zealand however the opportunity arose to go to Australia and Fiji and always being up for an adventure, we went. I am amazed at how well Fred did, now knowing he had a large tumor growing deep in his brain. It was truly a blessing that we did not know prior to the trip what was going on, as we would have either cancelled or been very depressed about what was to come. I am astounded that Fred didn't have seizures, was able to snorkel at The Great Barrier Reef, and didn't complain of any pain, though now there were signs such as extreme fatigue, but we thought it was just jet lag. As we sat on the beach in Fiji on his 63rd birthday, April 17th, 2016, we were treated to the most spectacular sunset we had ever seen. In fact, many locals commented it was the prettiest sunset they had ever seen as well. I don't think it was a coincidence, I really think it was a Heavenly gift as we talked about that sunset many times throughout Fred's illness. Words cannot describe how much I miss Fred, particularly today. He would have been 64 and I would have started planning a surprise 65th birthday party for him next year. Oddly, the tears haven't flowed as much as I had expected. The emotion expended this weekend as we buried Fred's mom maybe "took the edge off." I am grateful he was able to spend his first birthday in Heaven with both his mom and dad. Our earthly loss is a Heavenly gain. I am reminded daily to not take people I love for granted and to understand every day truly is a gift, and I need to treat is as such. Happy Birthday Fred! You will always be the love of my life.

May 4

An update from The Tar Pit. I knew this week would be a tough one and it did not "disappoint." One year ago, this past Saturday, we had a family trip to the zoo and it became frighteningly evident that something was very wrong with Fred. He knew something was wrong as well, and we all watched him looking confused and having difficulty keeping up with us walking. We still didn't know what was wrong though. One year ago, today I was sitting at the National Day of Prayer breakfast and it was all I could do to get through it without breaking down in tears. It was just the night before that I'd figured out he mostly likely had a brain tumor and we were working to get the MRI pre-certified to confirm the diagnosis. Each day he rapidly declined and by the weekend he would barely be able to walk.

Wow! What a year. I never imagined one year ago I would be a widow, the boys would be without their dad, we would lose a brother-in-law (Jerry) and Mom Rogers.

One year ago began the entrance into "The Tar Pit" and soon I would be working to stay afloat. Throughout my career, as I have worked with those going through grief, I would talk about The Tar Pit and I envisioned it more like a pond or lake that one struggled to get through, but would be able to see the other side, and eventually get out "on safe ground." Oh, was I wrong! It has become clear to me that "The Tar Pit" is really like the ocean, we can't see the other side until a great deal of travel through it has occurred, sometimes through rough waters and huge waves of sadness. Sometimes there is calm, but there is always the risk of becoming too fatigued and going under. Then, as we approach the shore and feel that we are nearing the safety of land, the undertow risk comes along. If we continue to swim and trudge along we make it to the shore, but I don't think we ever truly get out of it. We may walk along the shore, but the tide comes and goes, and sometimes we are pulled back in as large, unseen waves hit us. Once again we begin to work our way to shore. Once we stop long enough to catch our breath and look around, we are able to see many others in The Tar Pit "ocean" with us. This was my epiphany, that we ALL are in The Tar Pit and are at various stages of treading, swimming, going under, and then moving toward shore again throughout our lives. Some of us hang out on the shore but never really get out, some never get to shore but we all, as humans, are there in The Tar Pit. We all go through loss and grief, and that my friends is part of the human condition. Life is hard, it is good as well, but is filled with loss and disappointment. I don't say that in a hopeless and sad way. Instead, I find great comfort in knowing that there are others with me to help me stay afloat and keep me moving forward. I also hope that I, in turn, can throw a life line of sorts and help others move forward. We aren't alone in this path through The Tar Pit. (I still can't call it a journey because I think journeys should be fun and involve a great trip somewhere.) Soon our family will face the tough dates, the first brain biopsy, Mother's Day without Mom Rogers, Father's Day, summer birthdays and then September 22. It will be here before we know it but we are blessed to have God holding us up and so many family members and friends to support us. So, no matter where you might be in The Tar Pit, I pray that you are able to look around and use a lifeline to help you get to the shore.

May 11

A shout out to my beautiful mom in honor of Nurses' Week. She is a graduate of Samaritan Hospital School of Nursing. Very fitting to post this during Nurses' Week and so close to Mother's Day. She is the woman who inspired me to become a nurse. Even at 80 years old she was helping me care for Fred last year. I would not be the person I am today without Mom as my mentor, cheerleader, friend. She taught me how to be a wife, a mother, a nurse, and walk in faith. I am grateful to so many for the support throughout the past year and especially to Mom who has always been my rock. Mom, you are an amazing woman and I love you!!

May 12

Yesterday I posted a picture of Mom. Today I post Mom Schwan Rogers and Fred. This woman was amazing! Her life story is that of a great novel. She immediately treated me as one of her daughters when Fred and I got engaged. If I am half the Mother-in-law to Lisa and Michelle that she was to me, I have done well. I feel so blessed to have had her in my life for over 33 years. How fitting that she was with Fred for his first birthday in Heaven and he is with her for her first Mother's Day in Heaven. It is a comfort to know that because they had Jesus in their lives they are indeed together, and someday I get to see them again as well. So Happy Mother's Day Mom as you watch down on us.

May 26

Another first in this year of firsts: our first Firefighter Memorial service without Fred. Many years I stood looking at the line of firefighters with my handsome man across from me, in uniform. He wore Ashland FD, Mifflin FD, or Hayesville FD uniforms throughout his many years, always proud of his uniform and fellow firefighters. He loved the years when he also stood with Nicolaus and got a year or two with Christopher who volunteered for Jeromesville FD. Tonight, while he was not there physically, I felt his presence, and as Mark Abel spoke so eloquently of him, I cried but also beamed with pride. Nicolaus was standing across from me and my heart swelled, as I know his dad was smiling from above. Thank you to all in our firefighter family who gave hugs, prayers, a handshake, or held back tears as we spoke. You are truly our family! The pictures are from the service and the video is of Nicolaus ringing the bell. It was tough but such an honor. As I drove home tonight, I couldn't help but look at the gorgeous sunset. I think Fred was smiling down. As we reflect on the sacrifices of our men and women in the Armed services on this Memorial Day weekend, I also want to say thank you to our men and women who serve and have sacrificed in our emergency services, law enforcement and firefighting. May we all keep in mind what this holiday is about.

May 29

Several days ago, I was honored to spend the evening with some amazing nurses being recognized for excellence in the jobs they do at Samaritan Medical Center. While some in the audience were being celebrated there were others in attendance just for support. Today, as I stood watching the Memorial Day parade, there were some in the parade but a larger number of people were there for support. It reminds me that we can't always be first and some of us will never be "the winner" but we all can be "the cheerleader." And in being the cheerleader we become part of the winner's story. The world would be a better place if when we stood on the sidelines, we cheered a little more and celebrated those around us, and grumbled a little less (me included).

July 21

It has been a while since I updated from "The Tar Pit." Hard to believe one year ago we were seeing signs that the tumor was growing quickly. Fred and I took our last trip to the Finger Lakes region of NY state. We had visited there with Nicolaus when he was a toddler. We said we always wanted to go back, so that was the final vacation trip. Shortly after we got back, the repeat MRI gave us horrible news, the tumor was growing. Our only chance was another biopsy and a clinical trial.

I look back and wonder how we got through last year. It still takes my breath away like being sucker punched in the stomach.

The difference now is that I can look back throughout those truly horrible months and see grace and beauty despite all of the sadness. I am grateful for our last months together to treasure the seemingly mundane times. I am grateful for family and friends who held us up daily in their prayers, cards, kind words, etc.

"The Tar Pit" looks different to me now. I feel progress forward, and some days I actually feel sure footing. The rocks below me are still slippery but I am able to keep moving forward. There isn't one thing that I can attribute to the forward progress but I know that only with God's hand firmly around mine have I been able to keep moving forward.

So many changes have come this past year for not only me but the rest of the family. We are grateful for all the love and support we still have from so many.

Semi-retirement has been good for me. I still have a NP job but it is PRN; it gives me time to keep up on chores at home and yet allow me to still practice the craft that I love so much.

There is no magic formula for dealing with loss and doing the very difficult work through grief. I have no perfect plan; I can say that it has gotten more bearable and that I find joy in every day. I think Fred would have expected that of me. He had such a great sense of humor and he worked to keep me from taking myself too seriously throughout our entire marriage.

I look forward to see what the future holds for me. I could not begin to look past the sadness a year ago. I know there will be relapses but I know they will be shorter and not as deep. To my fellow "Tar pit" travelers, I keep you in my prayers. Truly, the only option is to move forward.

August 23

Update from The Tar Pit:

It's quickly coming, the end of the "year of firsts." As I reflect on the enormous changes we have faced as a family and friends I am truly amazed at how we made it this far. Words like difficult and painful and horrible don't seem to really capture the essence of it all. And yet, it has also been full of hope for the future and proof of the resilience of the human spirit.

So many of you have followed my posts from "The Tar Pit." As Fred and I started on this path in May of 2016 we discussed how we wanted to be the ones sharing the information and facts, and not have it come from many different sources. Thus, the postings began, first with Fred and I together as I typed the words but with him at my side. As he declined, he still was often by my side but was unable to articulate the words to share, and eventually it became me, with him still in my heart but not physically beside me any longer.

If it were not for my faith in eternity, salvation, and God, and support from family and friends, I truly would not have gotten more than a few steps into The Tar Pit. I certainly would not have had the peace, strength and hope to continue through it.

I have had people tell me they are happy I am "moving on" as I learn to reshape my life without Fred physically by my side. A piece of him will always live in my heart however. I think he would be very disappointed in me if I lingered too long in The Tar Pit filled with self-pity and desolation. He wasn't the kind of man to sit around and feel sorry for himself and he made me a better person in watching him for 32 years face all sorts of adversity with persistence and often a smile despite great difficulty surrounding him.

I don't see that I have "moved on," I see it as "pushing forward." Moving on seems trite and at times easy. I moved on as I graduated from high school and headed off to college. I moved on as I retired and headed off into new career opportunities. I missed the experiences but I was able to compartmentalize them, close the chapter, and head off to start the new one.

Pushing forward is more active, more deliberate, more difficult. For me it implies carrying the load and trudging through, in this case The Tar Pit, to get to a place of peace. I am pushing forward despite the hole in my heart which will never be filled but having the possibility of loving again. Because of the love I had with Fred was so amazing, taking a chance someday on love is worth it. Pushing forward is knowing that it will still be hard and laborious and messy sometimes.

So many of you have had losses and feel grief as much as me, and some more. What I understand is that life is not fair and we don't get to have the answers as to "why?." God didn't promise us easy or answers. He did however promise us eternity with Him if we believe in Christ and that He is the way to the Father. It is with that knowledge that I push forward, some days taking steps back but always knowing I have the strength through my Heavenly Father to continue forward. I hope those of you who struggle with the pain of loss and grief continue to find your way on the path through The Tar Pit and push forward.

September 17

As our family and friends enter a tough walk through the Tar Pit this week and deal with the first anniversary of Fred's death, I do not think it was a coincidence that my devotionals were about the Kerith Ravine.

The Kerith Ravine is where the prophet Elijah was told to go. Once there he was fed in the morning and the evening by ravens. Ravens are not known for being nurturing so this makes this even more unusual. The rest pf the region was in the midst of a drought, and yet, a cool brook provided Elijah with water. All of this was to show how God provides in hardship. Elijah was hiding from King Ahab who he had angered for telling him that he was evil in the eyes of God. If we stop and listen, God provides our strength and refuels us for difficulties in our lives. May you find peace in all the difficulties you face.

September 20

Update from The Tar Pit. As many of you know, September 22 will be one year since Fred died. As the date approached, I wondered how I would handle it and what I would do. I thought of so many people Fred touched in his short 63 years on this earth and certainly felt the loss for the boys, Fred's sisters, and the rest of the family as well as friends. I thought of Fred in Heaven with his mom and dad. What joy they must be experiencing together!

The walk through The Tar Pit has been long, difficult, messy, painful, and yet, it has been one of rebirth and grace. I would never have chosen this path-EVER and yet, in an odd way it has been a gift. It has made me much more aware of the many blessings I have been given in my life. It has caused me to leave my comfort zone and publicly share my walk of faith in God and Jesus Christ. I have had a deep faith for years but rarely talked openly and so publicly. It has allowed me to connect with others on a different level, particularly many of my patients who have experienced great losses and the gift of presence and compassion with my fellow humans is priceless.

Throughout the year and a-half since Fred's diagnosis and subsequent death, I was given such support and encouragement. From the first FB post through now, I have been asked by many people to continue to post. It felt very uncomfortable at first but as I continued, I felt a much deeper connection with God. Truly, if it were not for my faith, I could not have gotten through this.

The walk through The Tar Pit has also brought my family closer together and the friendship and love we have experienced from so many people is humbling and overwhelming. I keep getting asked if I have started my book and the answer is "yes." I have 5 chapters in draft and will keep writing. Once I get it published, I will get the word out.

I thought about what to write as an update this week. I recently posted a picture of a lighthouse and how the scars we reveal give light to others like a lighthouse to those who are headed for the same rocks. Many of you have been my lighthouse as I watched you walk through The Tar Pit ahead of me. Your forward progress gave me hope and light.

Tar Pit dwelling is dangerous; it is a place we all will need to eventually enter to deal fully with our grief. The choice to not enter means it is a choice to live with unresolved grief. Once we travel a bit in The Tar Pit we become like buoys to other Tar Pit dwellers. The buoy helps hold up those who need to rest awhile or to signal dangerous areas but the problem with remaining a buoy is that we never will make forward progress. We become stuck in The Tar Pit.

Continuing to remain deep in The Tar Pit can become "comfortable," not in a pleasant way, but in a "familiar" way. It becomes easier to stay put than to exert the energy to continue to push forward. As I have posted before, pushing forward is different than moving on. Pushing forward is difficult, messy and at times very painful. Just like a caterpillar that must undergo the work of metamorphosis and then the struggle to free itself from the chrysalis, we too must enter the struggle to push forward through The Tar Pit. I think most of us always live on the edge, once we get through "The Pit." We get pulled back in by another loss, or things like anniversary dates of events, but being on the edge gives rise to new beginnings.

The lighthouse metaphor struck home for me. As I trudged along this year, I really needed to see the light ahead. For those of you who have been my lighthouse, thank you! I hope I can be a lighthouse for others as they too trudge forward.

My next posting related to The Tar Pit will be the eulogy I wrote and read at Fred's funeral. I think it gave some insight into such a great part-ner, dad, brother, son, friend, uncle, grandfather, and many other roles he filled in our lives. I then will take some time away from Tar Pit postings for a while.

I thank you all for your ongoing love and support. You have truly been amazing gifts to me and my family.

September 21

One Year Later: The Tar Pit

As I posted yesterday, my last posting from The Tar Pit for a while will be the eulogy I wrote and read at Fred's funeral. So here it is.

On behalf of all of the family, I want to thank everyone in attendance, as well as those who could not be here, for the love, support, prayers, hugs, and words of encouragement and comfort. If it were not for all of that we would not have been able to walk this path. As I have said before, I am not calling it a journey as I think a journey should be fun and involve plane tickets.

There are so many things I want you all to know about Fred but there is not enough time or tissues for that so I will try to keep this as a reasonable tribute.

To all who knew Fred, you are keenly aware of his sense of humor. The first thing that comes to mind after his hairy body and his bald head will always be his sense of humor. He rarely took himself too seriously & he was very good at trying to keep everyone else, including me, from taking things too seriously as well. There was a side of Fred though that was very serious. If he was passionate about a topic, whether it was driving a fire engine the proper way, sweeping & waxing a floor, cleaning a toilet, folding his underwear & handkerchiefs, or eating ice cream, pizza or popcorn, you quickly knew that it was important to him.

He was even more passionate about his family, friends, & faith. I met Fred in February of 1984 while still relatively young in my nursing career. He was 8 years older, a firefighter/paramedic & he had lost his dad to cancer in 1982. We met as a blind date which consisted of stopping at a chimney fire on the way to a movie & then going to The Best Western just off route 30 to listen to the band. I remember sitting with Fred & Tom Workman & thinking that this was the most unusual first date I had ever been on.

I watched Fred interact with his mom, sisters, brothers-in-law, nieces & nephews, aunts

& uncles, & cousins as I met more & more of the family. I was so impressed with the love & devotion he had for them, particularly his mom, and how he had such wonderful memories of his dad. I knew this was the man I wanted to marry & spend the rest of my days with because I knew he would treat me & my family the same way. To say he exceeded my expectations is an understatement.

Little did I know that February 12, 1984, our first date, would be the beginning of a wonderful love story that ended way too soon; but what it lacked in quantity, it surpassed in quality. We began our partnership in traveling, in our professional careers, in raising a family & in becoming best friends who always had each other's back. When I wavered in my confidence to do something, Fred was always there to cheer me on & tell me it would be OK. When he would have a fatal fire or crash, or otherwise rough day at work, I was there to hug him & tell him we would get through it. And we always did.

This big, hairy, bald guy with massive bear paw hands had the biggest heart. If someone needed help, he was there. It is no wonder that our sons have followed in their father's footsteps to become public servants whether in the military, fire department, or law enforcement. Fred was a school volunteer, soccer coach, den leader for Cub Scouts, honorary FFA Alumni, worked concession stands, sold 50/50 tickets, & sold programs for many Hillsdale sporting events. He helped with set up & then during the annual FFA consignment auction for many years & even "donated" a finger for the cause the year he amputated his little finger. Not to worry though, it was re-attached. You could find Fred frequently at a fire department event whether for the Ashland, Hayesville-Vermillion, or Mifflin FD's. He worked the Firemen's tent at the Ashland fair for years, helped build the Fire Cabin, worked Pancake Day & volunteered in the clown unit as Freddie the Fire Duck for the Ashland Fire Co. Most recently he helped with the Mifflin Pancake breakfasts & Hayesville Kickball tournaments. Fred took the lead in the Ashland Community by rounding up food, water & supplies after Hurricane Andrew hit & found a way to ship it all to Florida. He regularly donated blood to the Red Cross up until the time of his diagnosis.

Fred put his knowledge of lawn & land-scaping to good use on the Building & Grounds committee at Trinity Lutheran Church for years. We teased each other that this Lutheran girl converted a Baptist boy. He was happy to attend church with me & raise our sons in faith; it was this faith that sustained us through many tough times including the loss of our beloved Dad Rogers only a few years ago. It was this faith that led us to Nairobi, Kenya on a mission trip & then to Ashville, NC with our youngest son, Christopher. Fred did not have a chance to go to Ethiopia with me but he was always there at "zero dark thirty" helping us load luggage & driving the team to the airport & was there to pick us after a long & arduous flight home.

None of us is perfect, and Fred is no exception. He was opinionated, stubborn, & could be snarky. Many times that was just as loveable in its own way. Up until the end, Fred kept his quick wit & charm. When I turned 40, I was not embracing the 40's at all. On my birthday,

after I had been working in the flower beds &
was hot & sweaty, Fred came home about 6:00
pm & asked if I wanted to do something special
for my birthday & I said "no." He was so mad at
me that he barely spoke to me for about 2 weeks,
the only time that ever happened in our 32 years
together. He would never tell me what he had
planned & I am convinced he was going to "wing
it." I asked him right before he lost consciousness
if he would tell me what the surprise was for my
40th BD before he died, he smiled and said "no, I
don't remember." Well played Fred Schwan, well
played.

While we are all sad about Fred's passing,
we know that he has passed on to his Heavenly
Father. It is a life well lived, but certainly far too
short. We talked many times about our thoughts
on life & death, I suppose it was because we both
have seen so much of it in our careers. Neither of
us had feared death due to our faith in the resurrection of Jesus Christ & the promise of eternal
life; however, we did hope to have a "kind death"
without much suffering. We are blessed that he
remained relatively pain free throughout most of
the cancer path; however, the last few days for
him were hard fought. Three people have taught
me how to face death with dignity & grace in
my life, my Uncle Martin Wolf, Dad Rogers, &
Fred. To say I have been humbled by how they
faced & accepted death is an understatement.
For Fred and me it has always been about the
quality of life & not the length of it; I must admit
though, I am greedy, I had the quality with him
but I wanted more quantity as well.

To family, thank you for your love & support to Fred, me, Nicolaus & Lisa, & Christopher

& Michelle as your siblings, nieces & nephews, son & daughter, uncle & aunt, grandchildren, & cousins. To Mom Rogers, Barb & Jim, Teresa & Jerry, & Pat, I thank you for sharing Fred with me & the boys & "our girls." You are a class act. To the AFD, thank you for your appreciation of "The Cap" even through his sometimes crustiness, he loved you all as brothers & some of you as sons. To the Hayesville & Mifflin FD's, he proudly served with you as a volunteer, as that is where his fire roots were planted. To the community, members of Trinity, staff at Samaritan Hospital, those in the Hillsdale School district, the AHS Class of 1971 (and others), law enforcement, community fire departments, & so many, many others, thank you from the bottom of our hearts! You blessed us daily with support & you truly have no idea what that has meant to us.

Finally, to our sons, Nicolaus Frederick & Christopher Wayne, you were named after your father & you carry so much of your dad in you. I beam with pride when I look at you & the amazing men you have become. If you are half the friend, partner, husband, & father that your dad has been, you will go far in life & in your marriages. Lisa & Michelle, you are blessed but at times you will be frustrated. Your husbands are so much their father & thus have his passion, his occasional snarkiness, his quick wit, & his charm. You have married Schwan men & marrying a Schwan man was the best decision I have ever made. Jordyn & Eva, your time with Papa Schwan was way too short but know he proudly wore the title of Grandpa.

While we grieve for the loss of what we anticipated would lie ahead, let us not stay there long, for that makes us sad & bitter. Instead, let us smile as we remember & share some really great stories of a wonderful man & thank God for placing him in our lives. We will see him someday as we greet our Heavenly Father above.

So today, September 21, 2017, I miss this man as much as I did on September 22, 2016. I find though that the sharp pain of the loss has been replaced by a deep ache. There is more joy than sorrow now. The tears still come but not nearly as frequently or for as long. Healing is a process, sometimes slow and sometimes fast but a process nonetheless. The Tar Pit path is still ahead but it has gotten shallower and I see the edge as the path is lit before me from those who have been my lighthouse. To my fellow Tar Pit dwellers, press on, push forward, do not get stuck as a buoy, God has given us a life to live and to make a difference in the lives of others. A life well lived after loss is a tribute to those we miss.

November 12

On the heels of Veterans Day, as I read my devotionals this AM, they spoke to me even more than usual. Here an excerpt:

"Brightly colored sunsets and starry heavens, majestic mountains and shining seas, and fragrant fields and fresh-cut flowers are not even half as beautiful as a soul who is serving Jesus out of love, through the wear and tear of an ordinary, unpoetic life."—Frederick William Faber

I am humbled every time I thank a Vet or active military member for their service. They always reply with something similar to "It was my honor."

While we watch NFL players "take a knee" for their "cause" I think of so many in our neighborhoods who quietly serve their fellow man/woman. No matter our lot in life, we can serve each other and show what beautiful souls we are.

Have a great week and may your sunsets be beautiful and your soul even more so!

November 19

From the book *Jesus Calling:* "Enjoy the rhythm of life lived close to Me. You already know the ultimate destination of your journey: your entrance into heaven. So, keep your focus on the path just before you, leaving outcomes up to Me."

I started this book last year right after Fred died and am in the process of re-reading it. It is a daily devotional book and has been a source of strength.

I marked the page last year and again today it spoke to me so I thought I would share. Have a blessed Sunday.

November 19

As we enter the week of Thanksgiving, I pause to really let it soak in how blessed I have been despite loss, sadness and pain.

Fred and I were given 2 amazing sons and while we did many things as a family of 4, Fred and I tried to spend one-on-one time with the boys. That bond has been a great source of strength for us, particularly the past 18 months.

I have many pictures from special times I had with the boys when each of them did special adventures with me. Christopher and I went hiking in the mountains around Tucson before he deployed to Afghanistan. Nicolaus and I hiked Yosemite several times and Mammoth Mountain in California.

I know I would have enjoyed raising a daughter but I think God knew what He was doing when He gave me sons.

Feeling grateful!

November 24

Ah… I get it. An excerpt from "Jesus Calling…

"Thankfulness opens your heart to My Presence and your mind to My thoughts. You may still be in the same place, with the same set of circumstances, but it is as if a light has been switched on, enabling you to see from My perspective. It is this Light of My Presence that removes the sting from adversity."

It is all about our perspective.

November 30

From today's devotional. I thought it was appropriate as we look toward 2018.

"Leave the irreparable past in His hands, and step out into the irresistible future with Him." Oswald Chambers

I think we sometimes drag our baggage of the "irreparable past" along with us and we fail to enjoy our "irresistible future" because we are so burdened and weighed down. I am guilty as well. God asks that we give our burdens to him and he will lighten the load. We cannot change the past; we can however learn from it.

December 3

An update from The Tar Pit.

It's been awhile since I posted from The Tar Pit. I've had an interesting few days of dramatic contrasts. I have friends and family who just have marked or will be marking significant "milestones" in their walk in The Tar Pit ahead of me. My brother-in-law, who died one month prior to Fred, would have had a birthday Friday. My-sister-in-law, Teresa Schwan Kowalski stepped into The Tar Pit ahead of me and I watched her "soldier on" with dignity. Several former co-workers face the anniversary of their spouse's death soon, they too stepped in ahead of me. Last night I chatted with a friend who is facing the "firsts" throughout his walk in The Tar Pit and Christmas will hit very hard for him. Other friends have been ahead of me for years through their Tar Pit walk and Christmas is always particularly painful for them. I think the combination of longer periods of darkness, generally cold and miserable weather, and all the Christmas cheer telling us we should be happy makes those in The Tar Pit especially vulnerable this time of year. I took the opportunity today as I got in what is nearly the last of a beautifully sunny and relatively warm walk to do a "self-check" on where I am and where I think I am headed through "The Pit."

I need to back up a day since my devotionals yesterday and church service last night really were the starting points for my contemplation about how I am actually doing.

I am simply amazed that when I take the time to quiet my thoughts and allow God to enter into my heart how He has the words I need for that day. An excerpt from "Jesus Calling" yesterday.

"I am the Prince of Peace... When you keep your focus on Me, you experience both My Presence and My Peace... You need My Peace each moment to accomplish My purposes in your life. Sometimes you are tempted to take shortcuts in order to reach your goal as quickly as possible. But if the shortcut requires turning your back on my Peaceful Presence, you must choose the longer route. Walk with Me along paths of Peace; enjoy the journey in My Presence."

I am so guilty of going off on my own and trying to get through the task at hand, including the grieving process. I do not like being in The Tar Pit and I really want to leave it. But, and there always seems to be a BUT, the path through the Tar Pit is partially on our timeline but also on God's. He expects us to hold fast to His hand and He will lead us through it; sometimes it takes longer than we want. I get into trouble when I let go of His hand and decide I am going at my pace without asking what God has planned for the walk. As long as I remain in His Peaceful Presence I do pretty well, and interestingly I have the strength to offer a hand to a fellow Tar Pit dweller. When I try to hurry the pace, I become unsettled, scared, worrisome and don't notice those who may need a hand at that particular time.

I finished the passage from "Jesus Calling" yesterday and moved to the next book I read from daily entitled "Streams in the Desert" by L.B. Cowman. This book was given to me by the co-owner of a bed and breakfast Fred and I stayed at in New York last July, as we celebrated the end of his chemo and radiation. Every day we were there I could see him declining and I spent the evenings after he fell asleep downstairs in the Drawing Room crying so he could not hear me. I was scared, and so alone, or so I thought. Gerry, the woman who gave me the book, would stop and sit quietly with me, as I cried, and she prayed with me. She truly was an angel on earth sent from God.

Here is the excerpt I read yesterday:

"Steel is the product of iron plus fire. Soil is rock plus heat and the crushing of glaciers. Linen is flax plus the water that cleans it, the comb that separates it, the flail that pounds it, and the shuttle that weaves it. In the same way, the development of human character requires a plus attached to it, for great character is made not through luxurious living but through suffering... Suffering is a wonderful fertilizer for the roots of character. The great objective of this life is character, for it is the only thing we can carry with us into eternity. And gaining as much of the highest character possible is the purpose of our trials."

And there it was!!!! All the "poor me or why me" conversations I might have with God really are answered above. This life is not about easy, or happy, or pleasant, although those are all very nice. There were never promises that we would get what we wanted. In fact, there never was a promise about this life at all. The Promise comes in the form of God who came to earth as a baby, The Christ Jesus. The Promise is that of salvation and the possibility of eternity with God.

So there it was, a lighthouse moment for me as a stood in The Tar Pit. I have The Promise and as I wait with an open heart through the Advent season for the coming of the Christ Child. It is that Promise which gives me hope and strength to forge ahead. It does not bring Fred back. It does not give me more time to share a life here on earth with a really great guy, but I am assured of eternity with God and the possibility of being with Fred, and all those loved ones who have gone before me in Heaven as well.

So yes, the Christmas season will always be just a little bittersweet and yet it is a glorious reminder of The Promise and if I sit still quietly, I will gain the strength through His Peaceful Presence as I continue through The Pit.

December 16

From my morning devotional. This is why we wait for The Christ Child during Advent season:

"These things I have spoken to you so that in Me you may have peace. In the world you have tribulation, but take courage; I have overcome the world."

—John 16:33

Jesus said this the night before He died. I cannot imagine His anguish of knowing what He would endure. When I pause to reflect on His pain and suffering for our redemption it gives me strength through the really sticky and difficult times in The Tar Pit.

Facebook Posts 2018

*J*anuary 5

Today has been a day of cleaning, getting inside Christmas decorations put away, and continuing to purge years of "stuff" that not only was mine but Fred's and the boys'. I am sure my sons dread stopping at my house as I always have a pile of "treasures" for them.

It is bittersweet going through all the memories of so many years with Fred. Some tears today but more smiles than tears, and a few chuckles as well. If I did not have my faith, I truly would be completely distraught and have no hope.

I found a 1985 calendar Barb Chandler gave me with the all the family birthdays and anniversaries as a way to bring me into the Schwan family. I treasure it still. Fred and I were married in October 1984, so it was a perfect gift to start the new year. Each month has a prayer. I found solace as I read through the calendar and was amazed how young we all were in 1984/85 when I looked at the ages also listed in the calendar. Wow!

January's prayer: "Gentle Lord, we pray that You will guide us through the new year. You are our Shepherd and we know Your voice. Help us always to answer when You call and follow trustingly wherever You May lead. Direct our feet in paths of peace and righteousness. And when we walk through life's valleys, walk before us, Lord, to show us the way which leads to life eternal."

Fitting today as I hit a valley in "The Tar Pit" but as always I push forward and am grateful for still seeing the lighthouses ahead of me as I near the other side of The Pit.

January 24

I have received quite a few books, booklets, etc. from the time of Fred's diagnosis through now. As I read them, I find excerpts that are very powerful, not just as it relates to grief and loss, but also how I am to live a meaningful and grateful life. As I am reminded by God, we were never promised an easy life or one without pain. We are promised salvation and eternity with God through Christ Jesus. It certainly makes dealing with the pain and suffering on earth more bearable knowing we can look forward to something so much better than we can even imagine.

I believe though that while we are on earth, we are tasked with making it better for others. It is easy to become self-absorbed and dwell on what isn't going as we had planned for our lives.

Today's passage is from a booklet given to me entitled "Do everything you can…then leave the rest to God."

"It's hard to leave footprints in the sand when you're sitting down. How you spend your time every day is how you're spending your life. Are you engaged in activities and pursuits that matter, have meaning to you, and give value to others? Think about the footprints you're leaving behind for others to follow. Are you happy with

what they look like? Purposefully invest your precious time, and yourself, in worthwhile things."

February 18

Update from The Tar Pit:

I rarely get up thinking "today I'll post
from The Tar Pit." It really just happens and
something I hear or read leads to either a step
backward into The Pit, or I find myself taking
a major step forward. It is incredibly personal
to share my Tar Pit dwelling activities and not
really in my nature. I have always been one to
journal (in those periods of my life when I felt I
had the time) and write poetry, but sharing those
thoughts and feelings was never my intention. I
have received such inspiration from people who
have connected with my feelings though as I have
posted, so here it goes.

I usually attend Saturday Night Service
at Trinity Lutheran Church and last night was
no exception. This is the first weekend in Lent
and Pastor Riesen spoke of Christ's temptation
in the wilderness. I cannot do his sermon jus-
tice but suffice it to say that it was enlightening.
One of his points was that we ALL will be driven
to The Wilderness at some point in our lives. I
think I named my wilderness "The Tar Pit." We
don't go willingly to the wilderness; we may be
thrust there through loss of a loved one, a job,
addiction, tragedy, etc. Before we leave this earth
though, we all will dwell in the wilderness. It is at
that time that our true self will emerge.

Christ was "offered" by Satan to forgo the
walk to The Cross by the temptations. Christ

really didn't have to die, after all, He is God BUT He chose the walk to The Cross for us. When I stop and ponder that it is so overwhelming that I cannot contain my emotion. He knew how it was going to end, with His own very deep and personal suffering and yet, He chose us. When in our own personal wilderness, our true self emerges, and the question is, what will we choose? What "sword do we decide to die on" and "what is our personal Alamo"? Do we decide to walk away from God or to be drawn to Him? There was so much more to Pastor Riesen's sermon but I can't begin to share it as eloquently as did he last night.

Fast forward to today. I have become an early riser, much to my dismay! I also am a night owl so sleep is at a premium for me. My routine is to wake up, get a cup of coffee and settle in for my devotionals. I find that centers me on my day and when I don't do it I feel "off" the whole day. On Sunday mornings I usually watch Dr. Charles Stanley. Today was no exception and once again, God has a way of pulling me to the place He needs me to be at the time He knows I need to hear it.

Dr. Stanley's sermon was on discouragement vs. disappointment. At first it didn't seem intriguing however I quickly learned it was to be the message I needed to hear and it seems to be Part 2 of the wilderness story.

In life, we all will face disappointment, it is the response to something that failed or an expectation that didn't work out as we had planned. Disappointment is inevitable and unavoidable. So far so good… I am disappointed when I want to do something outside and it rains all day or when I bake bread and it doesn't rise correctly. Nothing deep so far…

Ah, but discouragement…it is the feeling of despair in response to our disappointment, it is a CHOICE. I never looked at it that way. We choose to be discouraged, and if we do, it begins a negative and downward spiral that can be difficult from which to recover.

Consequences of discouragement are many and here are a few. It divides our attention as we focus on everything that is wrong, and we fail to see anything good or feel joy. We lose confidence in the future, and many things suffer including our relationships with others. Discouragement breeds discontentment, and we develop a negative spirit, once again affecting our relationships with others, and most importantly with God. When we are discouraged we make unwise decisions and leave our minds open to temptation from Satan. Ah!!! here it was, the link to The Wilderness… The Tar Pit…

When we get into the wilderness of discouragement, and we will, how do we get out? First, we must look up to God. We were promised He would never leave us or forsake us, but we have to acknowledge that He is there, not for His sake, but for ours. We need to look back at God's faithfulness in the past. For those who can't see that God was ever with them, it will take a deep look inside to discover this one. And we must look to the future and what we can do with God by our side, trusting that He has a plan for us. (Very difficult for we control freaks.)

In Mark 6: 30–31 Jesus tells the disciples to come away from the crowds to rest, "Come aside by yourselves to a deserted place and rest awhile."

The verse goes on" For there were many coming and going, and they did not even have time to eat." This occurred shortly before the feeding of the 5,000. We need time to quietly contemplate. I think that is why I feel centered when I start my day with devotionals and feel unsettled when I don't. It helps to fight off my feelings of discouragement.

I may seem odd to think of Fred's death as a "disappointment." It seems too tragic that a really wonderful man died way too soon, and any of us who knew him can't help but miss him. If I go to the place that is discouragement though I begin the backward trek into the depths of The Tar Pit again. I think about what I lost vs. what I gained by having him in my life. I think about my sadness, instead of the joy we had, and how incredibly blessed I am that we had two amazing sons together. Being discouraged makes me sad at not getting 50 years of marriage with him, instead of realizing that 32 years with him was a gift.

And so today another step forward through The Tar Pit. As I move through the Lenten season, I will be reminded daily that Christ died for me…for us, sinners, each and every one. It is hard to be discouraged about the gift of salvation.

April 3

Now that Easter has passed, the hard part of living "the message" of The Resurrection begins. It is easy to feel good about eternity and getting past pain and suffering when the thought of Christ no longer on the cross is before us on Easter morning. It is in the day-to-day living that we see how well our faith is grounded.

I have rambling thoughts when I am out walking, particularly when my big dog is walking me. I work to keep in control as she finds a scent of a rabbit, skunk, deer, or "Hefalump." No matter how much I work with her on heeling, sitting, and staying, when she gets on a scent, she is all coon dog. She is true to herself and what she was created to be, that of a dog, a hunting dog to be specific.

I live in the country between fields that are full of beef cattle during the Spring through late Fall. Most of you who know me know I am a vegetarian. (This is not a commentary about carnivores.) I enjoy watching the cattle throughout the seasons. To be honest, I talk to those who are close to the fence as I walk the dog around the property several times per day. They sometimes run from this goofy lady who talks to them, and sometimes they just stand watching the dog and me as we make our rounds. My point being, they are beef cattle. They are here for one purpose and that is to become someone's meal at some point.

I suppose I should feel bad for them, knowing that they will most certainly go off to be processed into burgers, steaks, roasts, etc but I don't. I realize that if were not for the one purpose, to become food, they would not exist. They are fulfilling their ultimate purpose once they become someone's meal.

As I walked the dog amongst the surprise April snow yesterday, I thought of how Christ washed our sins away and covered us anew, just like the white snow covered everything. I thought about what our purpose on the earth is, and then how we define our purpose, just as the cattle have their primary purpose too. (My thoughts really ramble somedays on my walks!)

At some point in time if I had been asked "who and what are you?." I would have defined myself as a Christian, a wife, a mother, a daughter, a sister, an aunt, a nurse, an employee, a friend, etc. All of those were true at some point and some are still true. Those are descriptors of relationships with God, with other people, with an organization, etc.

All those relationships though, with the exception one, are temporary. We lose those we love to death, to divorce, to substance abuse, to time and distance, and the list goes on. We change jobs, we retire, we change vocations. Truly, the only thing we can count on into eternity is our relationship with God.

The Tar Pit is an "interesting" place. Within the past month I have had acquaintances and good friends lose parents, children, siblings, spouses and friends. Today I talked to a couple who still walk deeply in The Tar Pit years after losing their adult son. Their comment was "this wasn't supposed to happen, we aren't supposed to bury our children." We talked about loss and grief and then we all agreed that if it were not for the promise of eternity with God all hope would be lost. I don't think I could have boldly had that discussion with them 2 years ago.

Life is ephemeral, or fleeting. For some who are grieving, in physical pain or suffering in other ways, it seems that the suffering will never end. Fleeting doesn't come to mind at all when we are deep in the realms of suffering. However, in comparison to eternity, life on this earth, pain and suffering really are short-term.

While we are on earth, I think we really have only one purpose, just like the cattle in the field beside me. (And no, not to become food.) We have a primary purpose, just like my dog who is a hunting and sniffing machine. Our one consistent and constant in this brief life is to live for the glory of God. I know there are some reading this who do not have a faith in God. It is my hope and prayer that as you pass through the brief days leading to the end of life, you are given the spark that ignites your faith. That is what the Easter message is about year-round.

How we define ourselves in the end has little to do with what we do as a profession, if we have children or we don't, if we are married or we aren't. It does have to do with relationships, but the primary relationship that is vital is the one with God. Once we get that one firmed up everything else is a plus, but it isn't vital. For me that thought has been important as I trudge through The Tar Pit. I lost my definition of "wife" September 22, 2016 and if that is what I thought was most important relationship I could not have moved one step forward. The relationship I had then, and continue to strengthen with God still, has been the reason I get up each day and put one foot in front of the other. It is that relationship that allows me to be emotionally available to my sons, my "daughters," my granddaughters, my parents, and the rest of my very special family, my friends, and my patients.

Tar Pit dwelling isn't by choice, it is part of living. Beef cattle don't feel the pain of loss like we do, they fulfill their purpose though. Our purpose is to reflect God's love and that is the most important purpose of all.

For those of you who have recently stepped in to The Tar Pit please know you have people praying for you that you may never meet or know, at least on earth. Your relationship with God is the most important purpose you have on this earth. Please allow the rest of us to help keep you pushing forward as you gain your footing again.

May 31

As I have written previously, I do not plan on Tar Pit postings, they just seem to happen as the day (or night) progresses. Today is one of those days.

For anyone who knows me, you know I do not like to ask for help. I enjoy giving help but I really do not like to ask for it. That actually is a weakness for a variety of reasons.

I took on mowing the property at Fred's diagnosis 2 years ago and am grateful I had help while I concentrated on caring for him. We all know how it ended. I have been the primary "mower" since then. My dad and kids have helped but I have tried to be independent.

Yesterday, Miss Independent got the tractor completely stuck in mud. I worked for hours trying to rock it out, dig it out, put sand and boards under the tires to absolutely no avail. I had to admit I could not do it myself and I called Nicolaus. I felt stupid and angry with myself.

Today, both Nicolaus and Christopher came to my rescue and extricated my tractor. They teased me but they treated me kindly and with grace. In the end, I was shown once again that it is OK to ask for help. The real lesson though is deeper.

I am reminded that despite my best efforts, I cannot do it all by myself. I am reminded that it is OK to ask for help. Asking sooner than later is probably better so I don't make a bigger mess. I am also reminded that grace is a beautiful thing. The boys could have lectured me and made me feel stupid, instead they helped me and made me feel loved.

I think God expects the same from us. We cannot "do" life by ourselves, we need His help daily. When we have made a mess of our lives, we need to stop and ask for His guidance instead of doing our own thing. And God will always give us grace when we ask.

Thank you to my sons for rescuing me from the mess I made deep in mud. And thank you God for continuing to help me trudge through the thick and deep Tar Pit.

August 2

Many of you have read my Tar Pit postings and have supported me and our family so much, thank you! Today's devotional was amazing timing, just like God's love for us all.

"You brought my life up from the pit, O Lord my God… When my life was ebbing away, I remembered you, Lord, and my prayer rose to you."
—Jonah 2:6–7

August 12

An Update from The Tar Pit

As usual, Tar Pit postings aren't planned, the "spirit moves me" on days I post. Interestingly, I woke up early since the grandpups were needing a potty break outside at 5:00 AM, that was after the 2:00AM break as well. I must say, the stars and meteors were beautiful!

I was awake at 6:00AM when Charles Stanley came on so I tuned in. The first part of the sermon was on The Holy Spirit. Hum… THE Spirit moved me today.

Earlier this week I was simply miserable. I was grumpy, and surly, and really not fit to be around. I couldn't put my finger on why until I looked at the calendar. This was the week, 2 years ago, when we were getting news the brain tumor was growing with a vengeance, Fred was deteriorating, we were scheduling the next brain biopsy, praying for a miracle, and awaiting the birth of Miss Eva. Talk about a flood of emotions then and now.

I tried to be civil to those around me this week, but I must admit, I really wasn't fit to be around. To any who had contact with me, I apologize for not being at my best.

What does this have to do with The Holy Spirit? Well, The Holy Spirit is God's gift to us to help us do His will and support us and connect us to God. The Holy Spirit lives in each of us when we accept Jesus Christ as our personal Savior. Jesus did not tell us that The Holy Spirit makes our lives easier or less messy though.

When we are filled with The Holy Spirit we are able to deal with the circumstances in a hopeful manner, no matter how awful things are at the time.

"The Holy Spirit is not an impersonal force; He is the third Person of the trinity who empowers, convicts, guides, & comforts all believers" (excerpt from Charles Stanley's sermon). I certainly needed to hear about the comfort piece (and peace) today.

"To be filled with The Spirit means we have surrendered our lives to Him, acknowledging that He owns us and has the right to lead us" (Charles Stanley). That certainly takes the pressure off of what I am supposed to be doing in my life as I only need to listen to the guidance I receive. Of course, that means I need to turn off my "Karin voice" and listen to The Spirit's voice in my head. For a self-professed control freak that is easier said than done.

The next 6 weeks or so will be difficult. I think this year hits harder for many of us who knew and loved Fred than it did last year. I can say that I am moving through The Tar Pit and can see the shore. I am grateful for those of you who have walked beside me, those who give me guidance ahead in The Pit and from shore, those who follow behind and inspire me as well.

The book is moving along. The essays, not really chapters, are in the final edits from me and are being forwarded to a dear friend who has agreed to read them and tell me honestly if they are worthy of being assembled into book. I'll leave her anonymous for now as I didn't ask for permission yet to announce her name.

The boys and I have our annual visit scheduled to Schmidt's Sausage House for celebrating Fred and the funny, passionate, loving, and yes, slightly frustrating man he was and how he blessed us. We will laugh and cry, drink beer, and eat a huge cream puff. We will continue to push forward through The Tar Pit and continue to treasure our memories, but also enjoy making new ones with those we love. We will form new bonds and strengthen old ones.

The Spirit moves us through The Tar Pit. Please check out In Touch Ministries website for today's sermon. It is what this Tar Pit dweller needed today; He definitely heard my anguish and sent me what I needed. Have a blessed Sunday!

August 15

Part of my devotionals today were from Job 38. A powerful reminder that when we feel despair and are distraught God has a plan that we may never understand. The entire chapter is powerful. I am reminded how small I am and how great is our God. I am reminded that it is not my place to question God, and yet, He understands when we do, for we are mere mortals.

"Where were you when I laid the earth's foundation? Tell me if you understand. Who marked off its dimensions? Surely you know" Job 38:4–5

August 30

An update from The Tar Pit

Many times my postings are deep and thoughtful. Yesterday was a deep and dark day but today, oh today...

My work day morning routine starts early, though not as early as when I was commuting to Columbus. In case you haven't noticed, we are losing daylight at a rapid speed, so when I do chores in the morning it's still quite dark. As I approached the dog's kennel this AM I noticed something odd laying in her food dish, it was a dead, young opossum. I wasn't sure it was dead at first, being a opossum and all, but yes, it was incredibly dead. The dog was quite proud of her conquest. And while I like opossums, obviously this one was less bright than normal or it wouldn't have ventured into the dog's enclosure. After I walked the dog and extricated the carcass from the food dish, I ventured onto the task of filling the birdfeeders. As I opened the flap on one of them, I noticed something moving in the dim light and hesitated enough to see a large, no HUGE, mouse plastered up against the side of the feeder trying to hide. I tried scaring it out to no avail, so I walked away. When I came back it was gone, or so I thought, As I approached the feeder with my birdseed container in my hand, the mouse jumped up into the air from the sunflower it was perched on which was growing beside the feeder. I screamed and swatted at the sunflower. The mouse went flying. Good thing I have a strong heart.

I laughed at myself and thought that if Fred were alive, I would have left him a note to please take care of the opossum carcass and fill the birdfeeders. Instead, I dealt with the mouse and walked in the dark to dispose of the carcass so it wasn't close to the house and smelled of decay for days to weeks.

During office visits today I had a patient who I knew. She said, "Karin, you lost your husband too didn't you?" I said yes and asked how long it had been for her. She said "Oh, it will be 5 years in November." (We Tar Pit dwellers gauge so many things on timing of THE date.) She told me that she still missed her late husband and that she felt she always would. I told her I understood.

Then she laughed and told me of the things she had to learn when her husband died like how fill the car with gas and mow the lawn. I laughed and told her of my opossum and mouse adventure and how I have learned to put air in a car tire, run both of my tractors, use a variety of hand tools, and deal with other household "adventures." We smiled and hugged as we ended our visit.

In the darkness and thickness of The Tar Pit, I find a glimmer of hope and light some days. Other days it is much brighter. I have learned that dead opossums can teach me a great deal about myself; that pulling up my "Big Girl" panties and dealing with all the difficulty despite all the pain is really the only option. It doesn't mean I have to always like it though.

September 22

I took a photo of Fred on his birthday, his last one with us on earth. It was taken in Fiji, in front of an amazing sunset and was a portends of things to come. When I am sad, I look at this picture and imagine him saying, "I made it, it's beautiful, it's OK. I will be here when you get here in Heaven."

Two years, wow. I am not sure what I expected at this point walking on the path through The Tar Pit. Always being the over-planner, I think I expected to feel the pain less sharply and deeply. As I have said before, we are truly closest to God when we are on our knees. I have been both quite a bit, especially this week.

I realize that when I miss Fred the most, it is for selfish reasons. When I stop and think about it, he's in a glorious place with no pain and every need is met. He's with his parents, friends and family and his Heavenly Father. I wouldn't want him anywhere else when I view it from that perspective.

I hope he's proud of all of us as we keep walking on the path, and yes, some days are more difficult than others. I don't think today will involve much pushing forward on the path. Just breathing and trying to not get sucked too deeply into the Tar Pit will be the goal.

Tonight, I will toast him with a Jack and Coke and look up at the stars and know he's safely in his eternal home. I will continue to thank God daily for the time we had together, for giving us our amazing sons and now their families, for the love and support from family and friends, and for placing me in Fred's family which is mine forever. All-in-all, while sad today, I know I am very blessed.

September 26

Below is the essence of my being right now, my mantra. When I am at my lowest and when I am being extra whiny, I realize it is because life does not now look like what I had expected and planned. In reality, I have so much to be grateful for and I am truly blessed. It is certainly different than MY plan but it is GOD's plan, simply put, "it is what it is."

I will not say it is easy accepting my "new normal" as now "the normal," but I am trying every day to accept life for what it is, and God's blessings for what they are, gifts from God.

I am a stubborn woman though and not always a quicker learner...

On Holy Ground a Thought for Today: It Is
What It Is

I used to bite my tongue if I had just
complained about something, and someone
glibly remarked, "It is what it is." I wanted to
come back with, "But it shouldn't be that way!"
Apparently, no one asked my opinion on how the
world should be run!

In reality, there are many things in this
world that are beyond our control. Rather than
allowing those things—or people—to rob us of
our peace of mind, we would do better to accept
them as they are, and concentrate on what we
can change—mainly ourselves and our attitudes.
The Serenity Prayer was designed to help us do
just that:

"God grant me the serenity to accept
the things I cannot change, courage to change
the things I can, and the wisdom to know the
difference.

"Living one day at a time, enjoying one
moment at a time, accepting hardship as a path-
way to peace, taking as Jesus did, this sinful world
AS IT IS (emphasis added), not as I would have
it, trusting that you will make all things right, if
I surrender to your will, so that I may be reasonably happy in this life, and supremely happy with
You forever in the next." Reinhold Niebuhr

Are you struggling to accept some situation
of your life, or perhaps, another's behavior? For
today, ask God to help you to accept the things
that you are powerless to change. Pray for the
peace that comes with accepting that it is what
it is. Ask for strength, wisdom, and courage
to begin the changes that you yourself need to

make. Pray as Jesus did: "Not my will, but Yours be done." Trust that God will make all things right in the end.

"Why do you see the speck that is in your brother's eye, but do not see the log that is in your own eye? Or how can you say to your brother, 'Let me take the speck out of your eye,' when there is the log in your own eye? You hypocrite, first take the log out of your own eye, and then you will see clearly to take the speck out of your brother's eye." Matthew 7:3–5

And going a little further, he fell on the ground and prayed that, if it were possible, the hour would pass from him. And he said, 'Abba, Father, all things are possible for you. Remove this cup from me. Yet not what I will, but what you will.'" Mark 14:35–36 ESV

"Give thanks in all circumstances; for this is the will of God in Christ Jesus for you." 1 Thessalonians 5:18 ESV

October 19

October 20th, 1984 was the day I said "I do" to Fred Schwan. It happened to be Sweetest Day as well. I don't remember Sweetest Day prior to then, maybe I just wasn't paying attention.

The Tar Pit has been a little thicker this week but not as overwhelmingly sad as I expected. I have really tried to focus on the things that give me joy and for being grateful for my blessings.

Those who dwell in The Tar Pit understand that just trying to get through each day takes an incredible amount of energy, and focusing on the positive takes even more some days. The energy expenditure is worth it though; wallowing in self-pity in The Tar Pit has yet to improve my mood or the situation.

If I had not said "yes" 34 years ago, I wouldn't have the amazing family that I have now and I simply could not imagine life without them. I get to spend Grammie time tomorrow. If it were not for a "yes" on October 20th, 34 years ago, I would not have Miss J and Eva who bring me such joy. The "yes" brought me two amazing sons and now their beautiful and wonderful wives who are my daughters. If it were not for a "yes" all my Schwan/Chandler/Plank/Kowalski family would not be mine. I truly have so very much to be grateful for; I must admit though, it's difficult to not feel a little melancholy.

I have posted pictures of the sunsets from my property. This morning I was doing my devotionals and the colors in the sky caught my eye. I grabbed my camera and headed out in the brisk and crisp Autumn morning to take a few sunrise photos.

I paused to reflect that both the sunrise and the sunset views, from the same location, are beautiful and yet different. I noticed that when I looked at the sun directly it hurt my eyes and the photos weren't as clear. If I took the photo through the trees, the filtered sunlight allowed the camera to take a better photo. (Yes, I know you can buy filters for the lens.)

I thought about how endings and new beginnings can be beautiful and neither one negates the other. I was reminded that sometimes not knowing everything all at once that will happen in the future is probably better than seeing it all and being overwhelmed.

I've made it past year two, and am working my way through year 3 of the "new normal." Each sunset brings closure, and each sunrise brings new possibilities and both have beauty. I am trying to focus on each day for possibilities and not trying to see everything all at once. (Filtering can be a good thing for facing each day as it comes, as well as for cameras.) I will continue to make plans and lists and check tasks off; I have been wired that way for too long to completely stop. However, I will try to stop and enjoy more sunrises and sunsets and be grateful for what I had, what I have, and what the future will bring even though it's scary at times.

The view to the East at the end of my driveway is an interesting one. The road reminds me of our lives; it looks straight and safe and yet I know that hills and dips in the road are ahead that can cause problems if I am not paying attention when driving. If I pay attention though and take care, it's a beautiful drive in the morning when the sun is coming up.

So…tomorrow I face the day with a little bit of sadness but with more gratefulness than anything, and I hope it's an amazing sunrise. If not, I still have wonderful memories.

November 4

An interesting story about a maple tree in my backyard. Fred transplanted it years ago, along with an oak tree growing behind it in the backyard. We both enjoyed watching this tree leaf out in the Spring, look green and lush in the Summer, and break out bold with orange-red colors in the Fall.

I am not sure when exactly, but at some point, we noticed the tree taking the unusual shape you see, as if something took a bite out of the top. Fred was disappointed and frustrated. Every year after that point he said he was going to cut it down if he couldn't get it to fill out. However, that never happened. I enjoy this tree and smile when I look at the "bite" out of it at the top.

Since it finally quit raining Friday night, I have been able to enjoy being outside. Fall is my favorite season. I have been taking photos the past few days and took some of this tree.

I find it interesting that this same tree looks so very different depending on the angle and the sunlight. It made me think of each one of us and how we have our own thoughts and opinions, particularly with the elections coming on Tuesday. Perhaps we all need to reflect a little more on the uniqueness of each one of us and of our opinions. Maybe we need to understand that if we "walk around" an issue we may see unique perspectives, and being "open" to listening to views that may never agree with ours is OK. We can agree to disagree. We can dislike the views of our neighbors, friends, co-workers, and family, but we can still like each other.

As I walked around this tree this afternoon taking pictures, I thought about all the issues facing our society. Perhaps pausing to reflect, instead of planning our next attack with a guttural response (from any side of the aisle) would help us go a long way in our country and our world.

I am glad my tree is still standing; I love its unique qualities.

November 16

I am not sure what causes me to wake up at 3:00 am and stay awake other than my mind that I can't seem to turn off some days. Devotionals usually quell the restlessness and I can go back to sleep on days I don't work at the office. Today apparently was not that kind of day!

I have been working on editing the Facebook posts for my book as my essays are being edited by a friend. As I read through the 2018 posts this AM, I was struck by my journey through The Tar Pit this year. Faith, family, and friends are really the only way I have continued to push forward.

This week has been full of emotions for some reason. I can't think of a particular milestone date that should be causing my "unsettled" emotions; I will just chalk it up to a wave moving through The Pit.

While cooking for the Mediterranean Meal Planning topic this week for Diabetes Support Group, I spent a great deal of time in front of my kitchen window while standing at the sink. Since I have lived in this house for 28 years, I have spent a great deal of time in front of this window. For some reason though, the view from the window caught my eye this week. I had never really paused to enjoy the sunset view from the window. I watch the birds, the trees, and a variety of other "happenings" from the window, but I can't remember pausing to enjoy the sunset from that particular angle. It was lovely. I then thought of all the sunsets I have missed from that angle over the past 28 years.

I have been truly blessed in my career to have shared in the lives of many, many people.

Some were patients I cared for when I worked ICU/ED/The Cath Lab/Med-Surg/etc. Some were patients I met through diabetes education/ Diabetes Support Group. I have continued to be able to share with people in my Nurse Practitioner role in a variety of office settings. It is a gift I receive when people trust me enough to allow me to care for them. It is an honor to serve people.

This week I had several people who taught me valuable lessons about resilience and faith in the midst of loss and grief. I had some deep and meaningful discussions about how it is faith that gets us through The Tar Pit. It is our attitude that allows us to see "the good" when really bad things happen. It is through the difficult times that we cling to God and our faith to get us through when absolutely nothing else is available for a buoy in the deep and dark Tar Pit.

These are things I knew before, but I needed these people this week to remind me of what I know and see every day. So…back to the view from my kitchen window. It is sometimes in the mundane tasks and the familiarity of our surroundings that we often find the strength to keep pushing forward in The Tar Pit. I once again am grateful for those who hold me up and keep me going.

November 18

As many of you in the area know, we had quite an ice/rain/sleet event several days ago. The combination of the temperature hovering above and below freezing, and the many leaves still on the trees made matters worse. I awoke in the wee hours of Friday morning and thought I heard some unusual sounds. When I went out to do my chores, I found a "Winter Wonderland" of snow and ice on trees, and broken limbs all around my property.

Today I spent part of the morning cleaning the limbs from the yard that I was able to drag to the brush pile. I "chatted" with Fred as I drug the limbs and thought of how he would not be pleased that I have created new brush piles around the property. (I think the critters in the back appreciate their new homes amongst the brush piles though.)

I got up early today and watched Charles Stanley. The first half-hour he talked about Thanksgiving from the traditional holiday Thanksgiving perspective, as well as the general "being thankful" for all things standpoint.

As they say, "timing is everything." It was nice to hear the message of Thanksgiving and being reminded that the holiday isn't about food, it is about being grateful and thankful for the bounty of our lives. The real message from Charles Stanley was about being grateful in midst of difficulty, pain and sorrow because Jesus promised to always be with us and never to leave us or forsake us.

After devotionals (and my morning coffee), I headed out for chores and then began the yard clean-up. I was sad as I finished cutting rather large branches out of one of my big lilac bushes that had been broken. It was also sad to see so many really large branches that had been broken out of the pine trees we planted years ago.

My sadness changed to a feeling of amazement as I noticed a huge and an almost completely intact hornet nest hanging from one of the branches that had been damaged. I was grateful to be able to see it up close without a risk of being stung.

As I worked on my yard, I was grateful in being able bodied enough to cut the branches I could reach that needed taken down; and grateful I could drag them to the brush pile. I began to think about how thankful I was that I have men in my life who know how to use a chainsaw will help me complete the task of cleaning up the yard.

One huge limb is laying across my black raspberry patch. The berry patch needed some attention but this wasn't really what I had in mind as I planned what I needed to get done next Spring.

As I came up from the back of the property, the maple tree with the "bite" out of it stood stately in its place. It fared well in the storm because the leaves had already fallen. It made me think of when we are stripped to our core and lean on God instead of ourselves, we are able to withstand the storms of life. Many of the trees that were damaged were my large white pine trees. They are majestic, beautiful, and lush, but they are a soft wood. We can become "soft" when we are not made tougher through adversity.

And so my sadness in looking out across my property was turned to gratitude and gratefulness this morning. It was completely unanticipated and unplanned, but I must tell you, my heart is lighter because of my perspective, nothing really changed physically around the yard. The trees are still broken, the limbs are down, and real damage has occurred to my trees and bushes.

As we enter the week of Thanksgiving, I hope all of you find a reason the give thanks despite any sadness or worries going on around you.

November 26

This weekend I worked on getting my Christmas tree set up and decorated, and my outside decorations put out as well. I am sure many of you did the same. At least in Ohio, Sunday was the perfect day to be out and about doing lights, wreaths, etc.

I also got out the books I read at Christmas time when I switch up my devotional readings. One book is entitled "A Journey of Faith, Hope, and Love: Voices and Blessings from the Nativity Story." It is the Christmas story with additional writings which are interpretations of what those in the Christmas story may have been thinking, such as Mary, Joseph, the shepherds, etc. Those are "the voices" part of the book. It also has blessings included. The voices and blessings are written by Paige DeRuyscher. Amongst the words are beautiful artwork of Matt Kesler,

It is a unique book. I am not sure if it was a gift or I bought the book. This year it just seemed to speak to me. I took photos of the blessings and will post them periodically through Advent. I hope all of them, or at least one, inspire you and give you peace and strength as well as "speak" to you as they did me.

November 27

I had a great visit with two dear friends yesterday and today. I am so appreciative of the friendship I share with these ladies. One keeps me grounded with her honesty and the other is a lighthouse through The Tar Pit. I think we need both types of people in our lives.

When I got home today, I ventured outside in the snow to get my chores completed. I like the snow and enjoy Winter. I don't like ice-storms and blizzards but I appreciate the beauty of the snow as it covers the brown mud and leaves and makes everything look fresh and new.

As I filled water buckets for my "critters" I walked by the container on my patio where I plant the cold crops each Spring and Fall of spinach, kale and lettuce. I had pulled those crops and the container was bare and rather sad looking. The broken pine tree branches, at the back of my property, came to mind. I took the clippers to the brush piles and began to cut some of the branches to stick into my container. There are branches from white pine, blue spruce, scotch pine, mugo pine, crabapple and Russian olive. These are all trees and bushes we planted throughout the years. I added a few decorations. While it will never win a prize, it did make me smile.

I thought about how, as broken people, we can be made new and whole through Christ. I thought how the broken branches from the trees as a result of the recent storm now make me smile. Perhaps they will be a place for some of my songbirds to use as a refuge as they forage for their food.

I have a wooden bench with a Moose and Bear on it. This bench was made by another dear friend at least 15 years ago. I have a picture of the family on and around the bench that I sent out in Christmas cards at that time. I think the photo was taken Nicolaus' Freshman or Sophomore year. This bench has seen a great deal of weather: heat, cold, sun, rain, snow, ice. It was looking rather haggard and I was able to get several coats of sealant on it after a quick sanding prior to the cold weather setting in. Though it has years of wear on it, the sanding and sealing revived it and it looks nearly new. Interesting that it needed sanded with the rough edges removed to then be sealed and renewed. It reminds me that at times I need to come to my knees and place my rough edges before God to be sealed with His love.

The Tar Pit is a little deeper as the Christmas season approaches. I think it will always be this way and I suppose instead of fighting it, I just need to breathe deeply and trust that God will continue to walk through it with me.

November 30

Advent begins…and today is St. Andrew's Day. Andrew was the fisherman who believed and had faith that Jesus was The Christ, The Savior. He told his brother, Simon Peter, about his "discovery" and these 2 brothers, became disciples.

I cannot fathom the faith they had to have to follow Jesus through all the trials and tribulations, before and after the death of Jesus. Many of the disciples would be crucified for their faith.

They were not well-educated men; they did not need formal education to have faith that what they were seeing and feeling was The Truth. They were in the presence of The Messiah.

As we enter the Advent season may all of us experience deepening faith even though we live in a broken world.

December 2

Trust is sometimes difficult, particularly when we cannot see, feel, or hear the thing in which we are placing our trust.

Every year, as I enter into the Advent season, I am amazed at the trust Joseph had to have when he found out his betrothed, Mary, was with child. What a scandal! What great trust he put in the story the angel told him, that Mary was a virgin and would bear a son who would be The Savior. He trusted that the message he received was from God and he trusted enough to name his son, Jesus, as he was instructed.

As we continue in our Advent journey may we all have the trust that Joseph had as he faced a life altering decision…to simply trust that God was at work in his life.

December 3

It is easy to love someone who is loveable; it's a much more difficult task to love the unlovable. As much as I try to be loveable, there many times I am just plain surly and difficult. I am a sinner.

It's amazing that God loved us, loved me and you, enough to come down from His magnificent place in Heaven to be born as Jesus, in a lowly stable. How much He loves us to endure death on a cross for our salvation. It's more than I can fathom. Even at my best, I am unworthy and yet…the promise of Christmas reminds me that I am loved despite my surly and cranky days.

Merry Christmas and may you feel love always.

December 4

For most of my adult working life I worked easily 40 plus hours a week and generally closer to 50 plus was the routine. It seemed that the more I did, the more I needed to do. I love my nursing career and though there were some days and periods of time when I did not like the job I had, I never stopped being grateful that I went into nursing.

It's been interesting having some "down-time." I am still keeping busy but I find it so enjoyable to take my time in the morning with my devotionals instead of rushing to the next thing on my checklist.

I cherish special memories, pictures, and most importantly time with my family and friends. At the end of our lives, it will not be the work that holds our hands as we take our last breath, it will be our family and friends.

Advent is a good time to cherish those people that bring us joy, and our faith that sustains us.

December 6

Advent: a time of waiting and a time of wonder. For me, it is time to remember that no matter what, no matter how well things are going, or despite how painful it might be, God is there to hold my hand. Sometimes God holds my hand to slow me down, or stop me temporarily. Sometimes He is there to walk side by side with me and yes, sometimes He simply carries me when I am too weary to continue through The Tar Pit.

"Footprints in the Sand" is a very special poem for me and in recent years it has become even more meaningful. When Joshua and Jared Wolf were young, they got me a coffee mug with "Footprints in the Sand" on it for a Christmas gift. I still have that mug.

This picture of the beach at the water's edge reminds me of rocky paths that God smooths with His loving hand as He holds mine.

May your advent season be filled with wonder and awe and a sense that God waits with us for His Son.

December 10

Advent: time for waiting, and for listening as well. Today has been a long day; a trek back to home from being away at a conference. The conference was very good, the surroundings quite lovely, and the company of my sweet mom made it outstanding.

The winter storm along the East Coast would have made for a problem getting home if I had booked the flight to return home yesterday. Instead, I booked another day when I made the original plans, to enjoy some sun with Mom. That was a good call. Waiting made a huge difference.

I was going to walk the beach early this AM, but waited. Thankfully my waiting saved me from the torrential downpour that occurred.

Today, our ride to the airport was incredible. I pre-booked a shuttle for our round trip to/from the airport. We were in the hotel lobby early and were asked by 2 couples if we wanted to share a taxi. I thought about it so we could get to the airport early, but then…we waited for the shuttle.

Our driver, who I will call Clarence, was a jovial local island man. He sang us a song and we talked about his island. He asked what 3 things we were most thankful for, I answered faith, family, health. He said, "Ah, I sense you are spiritual."

This began an amazing discussion about how this 64-year-old Christian husband, father of 5 daughters, grandfather of 3, was transformed from a drug addicted, sexually immoral man.

At 19 his mother brought him a Bible. He said he couldn't get through Genesis, too many names and people dying. He later started on the New Testament and when he got to Christ's crucifixion he was moved to tears. He found Jesus that night but still continued in his wayward life. He stated he knew he was changed though. Then one day he simply gave up the drugs and sex and bad influences and accepted Christ as his savior. He later helped some of his friends find their way to God. He met his wife at church, it was love, not lust, at first sight. By now I have tears in my eyes.

We talked about faith and how it sustains us. He shared how he witnessed the death of his dad, a fire chief at the local airport. I shared my loss of Fred, my firefighter and that Nicolaus followed in his dad's footsteps. He has a daughter who is a cardiologist and one who starts academy soon to be a Police Officer. I shared I was a NP working in Cardiology and have a son who is a Police Officer. His comment, "isn't that interesting that we live so far away from each other and yet we have so much in common."

As we shook hands at the airport, it was a special good-bye.

I thought about how just waiting made all the difference in the day.

Have a peaceful Advent filled with meaningful waiting.

December 21

Advent: The last posting from the book "A Journey of Faith, Hope, and Love."

I saved Hope for this last posting for a reason. Hope for me is the very essence of the Christmas season. It is through the birth of the Christ Child that the world has Hope in salvation. We are unable to save ourselves.

If I did not have Hope in my future in Heaven and that God sustains me every day on earth, I would not be able to continue this path through The Tar Pit.

In almost 40 years in nursing, it has been the hope of seeing someone become well and leave the hospital, of seeing a baby born, and yes, of praying for death to come so pain and suffering would end, that sustained me day in and day out.

Children hope that they get what they want for Christmas. We adults hope we can get through the Christmas and New Year time with little weight gain, or with the ability to pay for all the gifts, or that Christmas will be magical for the little ones in our lives.

I think there is a striking difference between hope and Hope: hope on earth is temporary while Hope is that which only the birth of Christ provides for this broken world.

I often post sunrise pictures because, for me, they represent Hope from above. They symbolize the birth of a new day when we get a chance to praise God and have Hope that someday we will be with Him in eternity. The pictures also remind me that there is hope in the daylight getting longer soon, hope that Spring will come (eventually) and these barren trees will be filled with green leaves, and knowing that I get a "do-over" every day for correcting things I messed up the day before.

I pray that your journey through Advent to Christmas and beyond is one filled with fulfillment of those things you hope for, but most of all, I pray you are filled with HOPE.

December 31

As we head into the new year, most will hope to leave the difficult times behind and look forward to times when the load is lighter and easier; I am no different in my longing for the same. Today my devotional spoke to me as a reminder that just as we are at the end of this year and are about to enter a new one, life is about contrasts.

Shortly after Fred died, I began a consistent daily time of devotionals and prayer. I had a prayer life with Bible reading for years but I admit, at times it was "hit or miss." I found myself more willing to sit and be reflective and ask God for guidance during the difficult times, and thought "I've got this" during the easy times. God has a way of bringing us back to center and certainly that happened in 2016.

I have always been an active person, I enjoy being on the go and having multiple projects I am juggling at any given time. Maybe that is what drew me to nursing, for nurses must be good at multi-tasking. I recognize though, sometimes my constant activity drove Fred crazy. He learned to either ignore me, or perhaps he learned to be amused by me. During frenzied activity, many times I did, and still do, some fairly "entertaining" things.

Hitting the ground running in the mornings has been my style…until…the Fall of 2016. I found that I needed the quiet time to reflect and be still, and hear God's voice and His plan for the day. What a contrast! As I consistently took the time each morning to find His plan, and not mine, I was better equipped to face the day. I wish I could say my days were easier, but alas, they were not. What I found though is that I was better prepared to face and handle the difficulties ahead.

Along with my daily Bible reading, I usually have 3–4 books with one to two-page devotionals going. Daily Bread has been on my reading list for many years. This year included Kristin Armstrong's "Strength for the Climb" and I have referenced her several times. Her words speak to me often. I have pages "dogeared" and many things underlined and circled. Below is an excerpt.

"Did you imagine twelve months ago that you would ever survive this past year…? Without winter there is no spring. Without rain there can be no flowers. Without mourning we have no appreciation for singing. Enjoy your life in contrast… May you never forget your winter of the soul, but go forward with joy and purpose in the spirit of love."

Soon my day will be filled with appointments and a few errands before picking up the grands. My house, now quiet and filled with only the sound of my fingers on the keyboard, will be filled with little feet pattering, little voices asking for a snack, and the sounds of laughter and perhaps a few tears when Miss Eva goes down for her nap. The contrast reminds me that I need my quiet, centering, restoring times, but I also relish in the flurry of activity I surround myself in doing.

I wish 2019 is a wonderful year filled with joy, success, and fun for all of you and for me and my family. This middle-aged lady knows however, that it will also have times of pain, sorrow, and disappointment. The quiet reflections each morning sustain me and I pray that you find your "quiet place" as well. Happy New Year!

Fred's Eulogy
Written and Given by Karin Schwan

On behalf of the family; I want to thank everyone in attendance, as well as those who could not be here, for the support, love, prayers, hugs, and words of encouragement and comfort. If it were not for all of that, we would not have been able to walk this path. As I have said before, I am not calling it a journey, as I think a journey should be fun and involve plane tickets.

There are so many things I want you all to know about Fred, but there is not enough time or tissues for that, so I will try to keep this as a reasonable tribute.

To all who knew Fred, you are keenly aware of his sense of humor. The first thing that comes to mind, after his hairy body and his bald head, will always be his sense of humor. He rarely took himself too seriously, and he was very good at trying to keep everyone else, including me, from taking things too seriously as well. There was the side of Fred though, that was serious. If he was passionate about a topic, whether it was driving a fire engine the proper way; sweeping and waxing a floor; cleaning a toilet; folding his underwear and handkerchiefs; or eating ice cream, pizza, or popcorn, you quickly knew that it was important to him.

He was even more passionate about his family, friends, and faith. I met Fred in February of 1984, while still relatively young in my nursing career. He was over 8 years older, a firefighter/paramedic, and he had lost his dad to cancer in 1982. We met as a blind date which consisted of stopping at a chimney fire on the way to a movie, and then stopping at the Best Western bar just off of Route 30 on the way home to listen to the band. Tom Workman, a fellow Ashland City Firefighter, happened to be there. I remember sitting between Fred and Tom and thinking this was the most unusual first date I had ever experienced.

I watched Fred interact with is mom, sisters, brothers-in-law, nieces and nephews, aunts and uncles, and cousins as I met more and more of his family. I was so impressed with the love and devotion he had for them, particularly his mom, and how he had such wonderful memories and stories of his dad. I quickly knew this was the man I wanted to marry and spend the rest of my days with, because I knew he would treat me and my family the same way. To say he exceeded my expectations is an understatement!

Little did I know that February 12, 1984, our first date, would be the beginning of a wonderful love story that would end way too soon; but what it lacked in quantity, it surpassed in quality. We began our partnership in traveling, our professional careers, in raising a family, and becoming best friends who always had each other's back. When I waivered in my confidence to do something, Fred was always there to cheer me on and tell me it would be OK. When he would have a fatal fire or crash, or otherwise rough shift at work, I was there to hug him and tell him we would get through it, and we always did.

This big, hairy, bald guy with massive bear-paw hands, had the biggest, most generous heart. If someone needed help, he was there. It is no wonder that our sons have followed in their father's footsteps to become public servants, whether in the military, fire department, or law enforcement. Fred was a school volunteer, soccer coach, den leader for Cub Scouts, and honorary FFA Alumni member. He worked concession stands, 50/50 ticket sales and sold programs for many Hillsdale sporting events. He helped with the set-up and then during the annual FFA consignment auction for many years; and even "donated" a finger for the cause the year he amputated his little finger on a piece of equipment. Not to worry though, it was re-attached. You could find Fred frequently at a fire department event for Ashland, Hayesville, or Mifflin Fire Departments. He worked the Firemen's tent at the Ashland Co. Fair for many years, set-up and worked Pancake Day at Ashland FD, helped to build the Ashland Fire Co. cabin, and volunteered in the clown unit as Freddie the Fire Duck for the Ashland Fire Company. Most recently he helped with Mifflin FD Pancake Day and Hayesville FD Kickball Tournaments. Fred took the lead in the Ashland community after Hurricane Andrew hit Florida by rounding up food, water, and supplies, and secured a way to ship it to Florida to those in need. He regularly donated blood to the American Red Cross up until the time of his diagnosis.

Fred put his knowledge of lawn and landscaping to good use on the Building and Grounds

Committee of Trinity Lutheran Church for years. We teased each other that this Lutheran girl converted a Baptist boy. He was happy to attend church with me and raise our sons in faith. It was this faith that sustained us through many tough times, including the loss of our beloved Dad Rogers only a few years ago. It was this faith that led us to Nairobi, Kenya on a mission trip and to Ashville, NC with Trinity youth, including our youngest son, Christopher. Fred did not have a chance to go to Ethiopia with me, but he was always there at "zero dark thirty," helping us load luggage and driving the team to the airport, and was there to pick us up after a long and arduous flight home.

None of us is perfect, and Fred is no exception. He was opinionated, stubborn, and could be as snarky as anyone. Many times, that was just as loveable in its own way. Up until the end, Fred kept his quick wit and charm. When I turned 40, I was not embracing the 40's at all. On my birthday, after I had been working in the flower beds and was hot and sweaty, Fred came home about 6:00 pm. He asked if I wanted to do something for my birthday, and I said "no." He was so mad at me; he didn't speak to me for days, the only time that ever happened in over 32 years together. He would never tell me what he had planned for that night; I am convinced he was going to "wing it." I asked him right before he lost consciousness if he would tell me what the surprise was for my fortieth birthday before he died. He smiled and said "No, I don't remember." Well played Fred Schwan, well played!

While we are all sad about Fred's passing, we know that he has passed on to his Heavenly

Father. It is a life well-lived, but certainly far too short. We talked many times about our thoughts on life and death; I suppose it was because we both have seen so much in our careers. Neither of us feared death due to our faith in the resurrection of Jesus Christ and eternal life. However, we did hope to have a "kind death" without much suffering. We are blessed that Fred remained relatively comfortable throughout most of his cancer path, however, that last few days for him were hard fought and difficult. Three people have taught me how to face death with grace and dignity in my life: my Uncle Martin Wolf, Dad Rogers, and Fred. To say I have been humbled by how they faced and accepted death is an understatement. For Fred and me, it has always been about the quality of life and not the length of it; I must admit though, I am greedy. I had the quality with him, but I wanted more quantity as well.

To family, thank you for your love and support to Fred, me, Nicolaus, Lisa, Christopher, and Michelle, as your siblings, nieces and nephews, son and daughter, uncle and aunt, grandchildren and cousins. To Mom Schwan Rogers, Barb and Jim, Teresa and Jerry, and Pat, I thank you for sharing Fred with me and the boys and "our girls." You are a class act. To the AFD, thank you for your appreciation of "The Cap." Even through his sometimes crustiness, he loved you all as brothers, and some of you as sons. To Hayesville and Mifflin Fire Departments, he proudly served with you as a volunteer, as that is where his fire roots were planted. To the community, members of Trinity, staff at Samaritan Hospital, those in Hillsdale School district, the AHS class of 1971 (and others), law enforcement, local fire departments, and so many, many other friends, thank you from the bottom of our hearts! You blessed us daily with support, and you truly have no idea what that has meant to us.

Finally, to our sons, Nicolaus Frederick and Christopher Wayne, you were named after your father and you carry so much of your dad in you. I beam with pride when I look at you and the amazing men you have become. If you are half the friend, partner, husband, and father that your dad has been, you will go far in life and in your marriages. Lisa and Michelle, you are blessed, but at times you will be frustrated. Your husbands are so much their father and as such, they have his passion, his occasional snarkiness, his quick wit, and charm. You have married Schwan men, and marrying a Schwan man was the best decision I have ever made. Jordyn and Eva, your time with Papa Schwan was way too short, but know that he proudly wore the title of Grandpa.

While we grieve for the loss of what we anticipated would lie ahead, let us not stay there long, for that makes us sad and bitter. Instead, let us smile as we remember and share some really great stories of a wonderful man, and thank God for placing him in our lives. We will all see him someday as we greet our Heavenly Father above.

EPILOGUE

As I wrapped up this project of love on the anniversary date of Fred's death, I thought a great deal about what my goal was for all the writing and emoting involved. Trying to capture the feelings of being a "Tar Pit" dweller was exhausting at times but also very cathartic and healing. Looking back on the path over the past two years has been difficult, and yet it gives me hope. Now, when facing something really crummy, I can reflect that I have made it through one of the most difficult situations I will ever face.

It would be wonderful to know that it will only improve from here, that the pain of loss will ease, and someday, I will not have the deeply sad days I still experience. I don't think that is the case though. My experiences in dealing with other "Tar Pit" dwellers who have entered the pit ahead of me show that the deep pain will always exist. We may not feel the pain as often, but when we do, it is raw and sharp. This is important to remember so we can be kind to ourselves as well as to others when the pain is being felt. I find it very humbling.

Having never written a book before, I don't know what to expect or where I go from this point forward. This effort may be only shared with immediate family and close friends as another way to pay tribute to Fred and the really terrific man, husband, father, son, and friend he was to so many. I may find that this book lands in the hands of others who are experiencing similar thoughts and feelings and somehow feel "normal" because someone else feels the same way too.

If you are reading this book, thank you for taking the time to read it. My hope is that you either connected to the stories because you have felt the same way or that you better understand someone on the path through the Tar Pit. If you know Tar Pit dwellers, I hope this helps you to come along side of them on their path or cheer them on from the shore. Your gift may be that you are a lighthouse to others.

My prayer is that you have been inspired to either deepen your connection with God or develop one with Him. It is only through my faith that I have been able to keep stepping forward on the path through the Tar Pit.

Karin

The scars you share become lighthouses for other people who are headed for the same rocks you hit. (Author unknown)

ABOUT THE AUTHOR

Karin Schwan is, first and foremost, a child of God. It is this relationship that has sustained her, particularly as she faced the most difficult role she would ever face—that of a widow at age fifty-five. Watching the love of her life and father of her two amazing sons die from brain cancer was a new and unwanted role. Dealing with the pain of grief, Karin shared her experience with others through online journaling and was encouraged to write a book. Poetry, short stories, and journaling were not new as she started writing these during her middle school years. Writing for pleasure would be interrupted as she headed to nursing school after high school graduation. She then began her roles as a nurse, a firefighter's wife, mother and, eventually, grandmother. As a registered nurse and nurse practitioner, she was quite familiar with the dying process and death, but the death of a beloved spouse, friend, and life partner would forever change her relationship with God and bring an even deeper faith.

CPSIA information can be obtained
at www.ICGtesting.com
Printed in the USA
LVHW041904300320
651613LV00005B/275